1720 $4.00
12/18/18

MW00940931

Ducks, Deer & Dynamite

52 Weekly Devotions for Men

Joel McDaniel

Copyright © 2018 Joel McDaniel

All rights reserved

ISBN-13:978-1727515169

DEDICATION

To my dad, my model of a husband, a father and a man.

Acknowledgments

I want to thank the following people for making this devotional possible.

First, Michael Oxner and Trey Clifton. These two men are my oldest friends, and they play a significant part in this book. I look back on my life with you boys and laugh.

Next, my mom who never fussed at a kid who cleaned ducks in her laundry room and flung fish scales all over her backyard. Mom, you have been an example of love and grace.

I also want to thank my wife Kimberly who has served as my editor, muse and cheerleader. You kept encouraging me when I got frustrated. I love you.

Finally, I want to thank my daughters Kinsey and Kayla. One of my greatest joys as a dad has been experiencing God's creation with you two.

Introduction

First of all, this book is an attempt to illustrate biblical wisdom and truth through some of my experiences in the woods and on the water, but it is not an in-depth treatise of various biblical texts.

Second, I reference numerous people in my stories, but the ones that are used the most are my wife Kimberly, my twin daughters Kayla and Kinsey and my two oldest friends, Trey Clifton and Michael Oxner. I say that so you have a point of reference.

Finally, the stories I share are true. I make that statement because I once had someone in a church where I was serving tell me he could not believe that the tales I told in my sermons were factual. My response was that I came from a land where people were literally named Bubba; my senior class tried to get Mossy Oak Bottomland® Camo passed as our prom colors; tractors drove down Main Street with as much frequency as any car or truck; and school was cancelled on the opening day of deer season because no one would be in class. I said I had held back on some of the particulars of growing up in Brinkley, Arkansas, and he was welcome to make a pilgrimage with me to the Natural State to see for himself if what I said was true or not. He never went.

However, that exchange produced the idea of using various snippets of my past to illustrate biblical truths. It is my hope that you will find these enjoyable, believable and applicable.

Week 1
You Can't Make A Buck Out Of A Doe

Kinsey scrapping cotton before a deer hunt

Exodus 32:1-5 When the people saw that Moses delayed to come down from the mountain, the people gathered themselves together to Aaron and said to him, "Up, make us gods who shall go before us. As for this Moses, the man who brought us up out of the land of Egypt, we do not know what has become of him." So Aaron said to them, "Take off the rings of gold that are in the ears of your wives, your sons, and your daughters, and bring them to me." So all the people took off the rings of gold that were in their ears and brought them to Aaron. And he received the gold from their hand and fashioned it with a graving tool and made a golden calf. And they said, "These are your gods, O Israel, who brought you up out of the land of Egypt!" When Aaron saw this he built an altar before it. And Aaron made proclamation and said, "Tomorrow shall be a feast to the LORD."

One deer season my daughter Kinsey and I had the opportunity to hunt with some friends on their farm outside of Bethel, NC. The weather was beautiful, the accommodations comfortable, the deer plentiful, and the food outstanding. (Sunnyside Oyster Bar in Williamston is worth the wait.) Let me qualify that part about the deer – the does were plentiful. We saw 14 lady deer but not one buck. It didn't matter how long we looked through the binoculars, we could not make those little heads sprout horns.

That reminds me of a man in my hometown who got creative in his attempt to polish his reputation of being a buck slayer. I was sitting in the Tastee-Freeze one evening during deer season and in walked this guy that was known for being a rough character. He sat at the table across from me and asked how my hunting had been so far.

After I answered him, I did the polite thing and asked about his season. He said he had already shot a couple of nice bucks which surprised me because not many hunters were having any luck. When I inquired as to how he had had such great success, he went out to his truck and came back in with a set of antlers that had wood screws protruding from the base. When he saw I wasn't making the connection, he informed me that he shot does and then screwed those prosthetic horns to their heads and showed his buddies his "trophy bucks".

I don't know if this dude was telling the truth because I have a hard time believing someone didn't check the other end of the deer. Be that as it may, he was bragging about how creative he was in fooling his friends. But who was really fooling who?

Now consider Aaron's folly. He gets scared because Moses is gone, and the people are restless. Aaron takes their gold, makes a calf which they declare as their god and tries to remedy the situation by saying they are going to have a festival to the Lord. But you can't redeem the worship of an idol by adding a little "God". It's like that guy trying to turn a doe into a buck by screwing antlers into the skull. It's still a doe.

Think about your life for a minute. Are you adding a little "God" to dress things up? Are you playing some kind of moral shell game by doing a few outward things that are solely meant to fool others into thinking that you are something you really are not? Let's be authentic by living life on His terms. Anything else makes about as much sense as putting antlers on a doe.

Week 2
Your Sins Will Find You Out

Joshua 7:20-22 And Achan answered Joshua, "Truly, I have sinned against the LORD God of Israel, and this is what I did: when I saw among the spoil a beautiful cloak from Shinar, and 200 shekels of silver, and a bar of gold weighing 50 shekels, then I coveted them and took them. And see, they are hidden in the earth inside my tent with the silver underneath."

I have a love/hate relationship when it comes to visiting my hometown. I love it because my roots run deep in that area of the Arkansas Delta. I hate it because some new story seems to be unearthed every time my family and friends get together. Memories start to fly, and all of a sudden something is shared that I thought had been buried in the dusty recesses of yesterday.

Take for example, the time I sunk my dad's car. Michael Oxner and I were driving on a farm road after dove hunting one morning. It had been raining a lot, and a portion of the road was covered by water. I thought I could ease through it, but the car quickly became stuck. At least I thought we were stuck. When the car quit moving, I told Michael to get out and push. As he opened the back door of my dad's car, in rushed a muddy torrent. After stemming the flood by finally closing the door, Ox proceeded to roll down the window and jump into what we thought was a shin-deep pool. Instead Michael went up to his chest in a four-foot deep washout. The car wasn't stuck; it was semi-floating.

My boy swam to the front of the car and pushed it back until the tires hit solid ground. We opened the doors and trunk and bailed as much brown water as we could while using the full extent of our sixteen-year-old male brains to concoct a story we thought was plausible. Instead of the truth, we told my dad we wanted to bless him by shampooing the car's carpets.

Fast-forward eight years. I was home visiting my parents, and my dad and I went to eat with Michael at a fish house on the Cache River. During the course of our dinner conversation, Ox said, "Remember when we sank your daddy's car?" Upon hearing this, Daddy jumped up, pounded his fist on the table and yelled, "I knew you didn't shampoo my carpet!"

Here's what I learned that day – your sin will eventually come to the surface. Take Achan for example. The word of God was clear to the Israelites. Do not keep anything from Jericho for yourselves. But Achan saw some articles that caught his fancy, so he took them and hid them under his tent. However his sin became known, and he and his family paid the price.

We may think we're getting away with sin, but take it from me (and Achan), we aren't. He couldn't hide stolen goods, and I could not hide a flooded car forever.

Is there anything in your life that you wouldn't want people to know about? Are you willing to be honest with God?

Week 3
Worst Marriage Advice Ever

Kimberly and me

Ephesians 5:31 Therefore a man shall leave his father and mother and hold fast to his wife, and the two shall become one flesh.

When I drive back to the motherland, I pass a farm on I-40 between Wheatley and Brinkley where I received the worst bit of marital advice ever. Let me explain. The winter of '88 was the last hunting season of my bachelor life. Come July 29, 1989 I was to be married to Kimberly Goldsmith. Now don't get me wrong, I was (and still am) crazy for my sweetie, and I could not wait until our wedding day. But I was not sure how one balanced marriage and hunting season. I got my answer while goose hunting with an older friend.

This friend's farm always had a lot of geese, so when he asked me to join him, I jumped at the opportunity. While we were in a field burning powder at blues and snows, my friend looked over at me and said, "I hear you're getting married this summer. Now before you put a ring on the finger of that girl you need to have a meeting of the minds about hunting. She needs to know that she won't see much of you once the ducks start flying, and that's just the way it is." And for some stupid reason, I thought this sounded like good advice. However, after trying to implement said advice, Sweets quickly disabused me of my redneck notions. And to be honest, I'm glad she did because such thinking is neither biblical nor practical.

Outside of my relationship with Jesus, nothing is to take priority over my marriage. Not my hobbies, my work, my friends and, listen to me, NOT EVEN MY KIDS. That's one of the points of Ephesians 5:31 which is a direct quote from Genesis 2 that Jesus also used in the gospels of Matthew and Mark. It seems to me if God put something in the Bible I should pay attention to it. If He repeats Himself over four times (Gen. 2, Matt 19, Mark 10, Eph. 5), I really need to pay attention.

A lot of people only have half the picture when it comes to the concept of "one flesh". They believe that this simply points to the physical relationship between a husband and wife, but that's just a part of the picture. You start with the spiritual which then gives way to the emotional which then leads to the physical. As a man I have to touch Kimberly's soul and mind before I ever touch her body.

I hunt as often as I can, but it has taken the proper priority within my life. And you know what? Kimberly wants me to go because she is not competing with anything. And that's really the way it is.

Is there anything that you put ahead of your wife? Have you ever sat down with her and asked her for her thoughts about how you spend your free time? Over the years we have learned that sitting down with our calendars at the beginning of each month and tweaking the schedule prevents any misunderstandings and hurt feelings. This communicates that I value her and don't take her for granted when I am making plans.

Week 4
We All Need A Jethro

Drury Traylor, one of my "Jethros" growing up

Exodus 18

As men, especially American men, we've been indoctrinated with the idea of rugged individualism. Images of John Wayne staring down a vigilante group in *Big Jake* or Clint Eastwood's exchange with Ten Bears in *The Outlaw Josey Wales* capture our minds. Often we hear a statement like "He's a self-made man." This is perceived to be a badge of honor. There are even those who swear that the Bible says, "God helps those who help themselves." It does not. As much as we like the images and sayings, they are not anchored in biblical truth and therefore not at the core of real masculinity.

Consider Moses in Exodus 18. Some scholars estimate the nation of Israel numbered over one million at this time. This meant, according to verse 13, Moses was wearing himself out trying to cover all of the bases.

But something happened that changed his approach to how he was leading. Moses allowed Jethro to speak into his life.

Now why did Jethro speak out? He simply was concerned was for his son-in-law and for Israel. "You'll wear yourself out…" means to wither. In other words, "Moses, keep doing this and you'll dry up." Jethro helped Moses zero in on his priorities. He was called to represent the people to God and to corporately teach them God's word. But when he added peripheral issues, he weakened his attempt to fulfill his first calling. Jethro was used by God to re-focus Moses' energies so that he was more effective. And instead of getting angry at his father-in-law, Moses listened and adjusted.

What keeps a man from following Moses' example and inviting a Jethro to speak into his life? Here are four reasons:

1. Pride says, "I don't need anyone."
2. Fear says, "I don't trust anyone."
3. Laziness says, "I don't have time for anyone."
4. Shortsighted says, "I didn't know there was anyone."

Moses fell into the last category. He didn't seem to have considered that others could come around and bear the load. Thankfully he had a father-in-law like Jethro who saw the need in Moses' life and came alongside him by sharing some wisdom that radically changed the way Moses operated.

So what does a Jethro look like? Here are five qualities found within Exodus 18:

1. He is someone we know. Jethro and Moses had been together for 40 years.
2. He is someone we respect. Moses goes out and greets Jethro instead of waiting for Jethro to come to him. Within that culture to go out was to say in essence, "You are important to me."
3. He is someone we trust. Moses tells and shows Jethro everything. He doesn't hold back.
4. He is someone who is godly. (See verses 9-12 and 23.)
5. He is someone who will speak the truth. Jethro simply holds up the mirror and tells Moses that he has to change.

Who could be your Jethro? Who needs you to be his Jethro?

Week 5
Watch the Foxes

Song of Solomon 2:15 Catch the foxes for us, the little foxes that spoil the vineyards...

It's kind of weird to do a men's outdoor devotional based on a book of the Bible that is about marriage and intimacy. But stay with me because there is a God-given principle at work in this verse. What the lover is saying is that in order to keep the relationship healthy, attention must be given to the small things so that they do not become bigger issues. The concern is not that a large animal will burst through the hedge and trample the prized vines. The focus is on the small, seemingly insignificant fox that slips in undetected and begins nibbling at the grapes until it's too late to save the crop.

As outdoorsmen we pay attention to the details when it comes to our hunting and fishing equipment. We break down and clean our shotguns when we come out of the field. We rinse off tackle after a day on the water, replacing line and checking guides. Immediately after duck season, we wash waders, stuff them full of newspaper to wick away the moisture and hang them upside down until the next year. Why go to these lengths? Because it's the small things that make a difference between having equipment that performs and equipment that fails. Let that small rust spot remain, and you'll ruin a shotgun. If you don't wash the saltwater off, watch the corrosion eat up your reels. Keep your waders dirty and damp and see how dry you stay on opening day.

Now for a simple, yet important question. Are you giving the same attention to your wife, your children, your friends and your church family as your prized semi-auto or your spinning tackle or an expensive pair of boots? Are you watching the small things that can weaken and ultimately destroy your relationships? What are some small steps you can take to care for the people in your life that will be meaningful to them? Listen to Solomon and watch the foxes.

Week 6
Wading With Sharks

My girls and I fishing at Shark Island

II Corinthians 5:14 For the love of Christ controls us...

For many years, one of my family's favorite summer traditions was making the annual pilgrimage to Atlantic Beach for several days on the water. Some friends blessed us by giving us their condo while another friend usually adjusted his schedule so he could take us out on his boat.

One time, my buddy with the boat called and asked if the girls and I would like to go to Shark Island and fish for red drum. We gladly accepted the invitation, set our alarms for the next morning and went to bed dreaming of bent rods and screaming reels.

The scenes from that excursion are burned into my memory - the sunrise with pink and purple hues, porpoises playfully cutting in front of the bow and flying fish launching themselves in our wake. We arrived at the spot, disembarked and began getting the tackle ready. The reddish gold flashes in the water told us the drum were there, and we quickly found out they were hungry. I loved watching my girls laughing and shouting as they wrestled those monsters onto the shore.

The fish moved from the breakers into the shallows, so we made the move with them. While the twins waded through the shallows ripping baits into schools of reds, Kinsey suddenly screamed, jumped straight out of the water and made a beeline for me. At first, I thought a jellyfish or crab had tagged her, but I was wrong. Instead, a small sand shark had swum between her legs.

She stood by me for a minute as she weighed out her options. I looked down at her and asked what she wanted to do. She looked at me and said, "I'm going fishing." Then she marched right to the spot where she had last seen the shark. Shark or no shark, she wanted to tie into big drum. Her desire for fish compelled her to overcome her fear.

Can that be said of us when it comes to the love of Christ? How do the following facts regarding the Second Member of the Godhead affect us in our daily lives? He stepped into history, took on flesh, lived the perfect life, died in our place, paid our sin debt, conquered death and now intercedes for His people. Do these realities capture my soul, my affections, and my thoughts to the point that I am compelled to live in such a manner that all other desires, fears and expectations melt away? Or do I allow the "sand sharks" of this world to keep me away from the joy and soul satisfaction found in Christ? Let the sharks swim; I'm going fishing.

Week 7
Three-Wheelers Don't Float

Honda 110, circa mid-1980's

Ephesians 4:11-12 And he gave the apostles, the prophets, the evangelists, the shepherds and teachers, to equip the saints for the work of ministry, for building up the body of Christ...

I look back on all of the things Ox and I did as boys and laugh at some of our stupidity. If Darwin was correct, then we should have been weeded out of the gene pool a long time ago. And just for the record, I don't subscribe to that school of thought.

How dumb were we? Here's just one example. Michael and I had taken his Honda 110 3-wheeler (that's right three wheels - way before four-wheelers and side-by-sides) to an abandoned sand quarry to do some riding. The way into the pit was a little treacherous, but we managed to maneuver the machine to the bottom. We spent a couple of hours tearing up the sand and running through the shallow portion of the water that had collected.

I can't remember exactly what happened, but somehow the three-wheeler's engine died, so we tried to crank it back up by pulling on the start rope. That's right, no electric start button – just a good old rope that could sprain your arm when the compression didn't release. Our luck began to go bad when we pulled on the rope, and it broke. At first we didn't panic because we thought we would just push start it. The problem was the tires would not grab the sandy soil enough to turn the engine over. It was at this point we began to get creative in how we were going to get the ATV out of the pit.

Where we were riding had steep embankments so pushing the

Honda out was not an option. But on the other side of the pit was a gradual slope that provided an easy exit. The problem was a lot of water was in between us and the easy exit. That's when we got the bright idea that since the three-wheeler had balloon tires surely it would float. Yeah, that's the answer, we'll swim that sucker right to the other side. Brilliant! Nope, stupid. As soon as we got into deeper water, that joker did a roll and turned upside down on us, flooding the engine compartment.

So we did what we should have done in the first place – called Ox's grandpa Arque (pronounced RQ) to come get us and the ATV.

Here's the point. The three-wheeler was not designed to be a boat, and when we tried to use it in such a manner disaster struck. So it is with the church.

Many people think the church is supposed to meet their needs. Others believe it is just a place where you show up and check the religious box on your weekly to-do list. If you asked 100 people in the typical church on any given Sunday what the purpose of the church was, you'd get dozens of different answers.

Simply consider what the Bible says about the church – it is a place where we are equipped to do the ministry God has entrusted to us. By growing in our love for Him and then each other, we engage in His work His way for His glory. Period. To do anything else makes as much sense as floating a three-wheeler across a lake.

What is you view of church? Is it positive, negative, or neutral? Why did you answer the way you did? If you have not been in church, look for one that teaches the Bible and get plugged in there.

Week 8
The Yes and No of Being a Man

James 5:12 But above all, my brothers, do not swear, either by heaven or by earth or by any other oath, but let your "yes" be yes and your "no" be no, so that you may not fall under condemnation.

As a preacher's kid growing up in a small farming town, I had men in my dad's church make remarks about taking me hunting or fishing. Some meant what they said while others may have just been trying to make conversation. The problem is, as a kid, you don't understand that some adults say things they don't really mean. Consider the following memories.

Wardlaw's Orthodontics in Little Rock, Arkansas – I'm around 12 years of age and arrive for my appointment. Sitting in the waiting room is a guy from my hometown who immediately begins to talk with me about the upcoming hunting season. I'm just a kid. He's in his early 20's. To a preadolescent boy, he is practically a man. He's on his own; he has a job; he has a truck with custom wheels and loud pipes; he's had his picture in the local paper with big bucks he's shot. He seems to embody masculinity, so when he says he is going to take me hunting I believe him. He never does. This failure to follow through confuses me. Why would a man say he is going to do something and then not do it?

Same year, different scenario – two men in my dad's church said they were going to take me duck hunting. They followed through. I vividly remember the details of that trip. I only had a .410 single shot at the time so one of the guys brought an old 20 gauge for me to use. It was a bolt action, magazine fed, beat up excuse for a shotgun, but in my eyes it might as well have been a Browning Citori.

I remember one of them handing me a handful of yellow high brass shells for my gun. I remember the day was cloudy and cool. I remember them picking me up for an afternoon hunt in some flooded timber right off the Cache River outside of Cotton Plant. I remember we sat until evening in an old johnboat with a dozen decoys on the water and no quackers in the air. No matter, the trip was the hunt of a lifetime for a young boy and a lasting memory for a middle-aged man who, on that particular day, saw what it meant to be a person whose yes was yes.

Fast-forward three decades. I'm sitting in a deer stand with a young man that I had promised to take hunting. The date was neither convenient nor the weather appealing. No matter. The lesson I had learned in that johnboat as a twelve-year-old was ringing in my ears. When a man says he is taking you hunting, he takes you hunting. Let you yes be yes and your no be no.

Are you making sure that you keep your promises? Have you broken your word and need to clean up things?

Week 9
The Real Reason for Climate Change

John 14:6 Jesus said to him, "I am the way, and the truth, and the life. No one comes to the Father, except through me."

I have read and heard a lot of explanations as to why we are experiencing so-called climate change, but this one is the most creative. It's because of "Sputniks". Let me explain.

One year I was on a property in Tyrell Co. getting ready for the hunting season. As I was pulling equipment out of our trailer, a neighbor from across the road drove up to check on us. While we talked, the discussion turned to the weather which had been extreme in that part of North Carolina. During the summer months, they were so dry the corn was stunted. Then when it was almost harvest time, Hurricane Irene flooded whatever crop was worth cutting.

While telling us about some of the details surrounding Irene, our neighbor said, "I'll tell you why we've had weather like this. It's because of them Sputniks they've sent up in space. Those things are messing up our weather by running around the earth and then punching holes in the atmosphere when they fall back."

At first I thought he was kidding, but this old boy was serious. He sincerely believed that satellites somehow disrupted the natural order of things and then wreaked havoc with the atmospheric conditions when they fell out of orbit.

Now I don't share this story to make fun of our neighbor, but to show that sincerity of belief is not the litmus test of truth. This man sincerely believes satellites are the cause of hurricanes and drought, yet, as all of us know, he is wrong. Objective truth points to the fact that the weather is dictated by forces other than man-made space junk.

In our post-modern culture, the mantra is, "There is no truth, especially when it comes to spiritual matters." One set of beliefs is as good as another. Allah, Buddha, Jehovah, The Force, they're all the same. Yet Christ explicitly stated that He was the means by which humanity was rescued from sin and death. Christ never said He was one of multiple choices or even the best choice, but rather THE CHOICE. To paraphrase the great Christian thinker C.S. Lewis, for Jesus to have said the kind of things He said leaves us with one of three options. He was either stark raving mad, the ultimate conman, or He was who He said He was – the Second Member of the Godhead, the promised Messiah. Lord, lunatic or liar, that about sums it up.

So the next time you start wondering about the huge swings in the weather, remember they're not due to Sputnik. And when you hear all religions are the same, remember Christ didn't leave that open for interpretation.

How does Jesus's statement hit you? If it is true, what does that mean for your life?

Week 10
The Power of a Daddy

Dad laughing at my "Daisy Duke" waders

Philippians 4:9 What you have learned and received and heard and seen in me - practice these things, and the God of peace will be with you.

When I think of my dad, many memories come to mind: a picture of him at age 28 sitting on a basketball watching me play between his feet, a quick release three-point shot that almost always went in the hoop, and a love for history that he passed down to me. The day that stands out the most was the time he took me deer hunting when I was five.

Now let me clarify something - my dad does not hunt. Never has and never will. But he knew he had a son that wanted to get into the outdoors, so he made arrangements with one of the families in our church to take me to their deer camp.

Dad loaded me up in the family car one afternoon and drove down Highway 70 to the Fuller Deer Camp on the Cache River. Old Man Fuller greeted us in his red union suit when we arrived at the cabin where he was shooting pool with his sons. We spent the night, and the next morning Mr. Craig, who owned one of the best BBQ joints in the Arkansas Delta, fixed a huge breakfast. Then we hit the woods - me with my Daisy BB gun and my dad with a Louisville

Slugger. (I made him take the bat because he needed some kind of weapon.) We saw neither hide nor hair of a whitetail, but that didn't matter. What mattered was a dad taking his boy to the woods. And I loved it.

Fast-forward three decades. Opening day of the North Carolina youth turkey hunt, and I'm sitting under an oak in Bertie County with one of my girls waiting for a tom to fly down from his roost. He gobbles like crazy for 30 minutes, hits the ground about ten yards from our decoy and then walks into the woods...no shot. But that doesn't matter. What matters is watching the world come alive in the still dawn light with my daughter. What matters is feeling Kinsey tense up when she hears the turkey 40 yards away from us. What matters is taking her to eat BBQ at a hole-in-the-wall joint. What matters is grabbing a milk shake in Nashville as we drive back to Raleigh. And what matters is hearing my thirteen-year-old say, "Dad this has been a perfect day." Never underestimate the power of being a daddy. Thanks, Pop.

How would you describe your relationship with your dad? Close, distant, non-existent? How has that impacted you as a man? What would you do the same as your dad? What would you do different?

Week 11
The Loudness of Silence

Psalm 46:10 Be still and know that I am God.

It was one of those days that seemed perfect for deer hunting. The wind was cool enough to let me know fall had arrived. The sun was setting and casting shades of red, orange and pink across the sky. Squirrels were scampering behind me in the leaf litter looking for acorns, and a ground hog waddled in front of me searching for whatever ground hogs search for. And in the distance, over the gentle rustling of browning oak leaves, the sound of an ice cream truck endlessly played "Do Your Ears Hang Low?". A motorcycle with screaming pipes was followed by someone blaring music so loud I could pick out the lyrics.

As I sat there dealing with these obnoxious intrusions into my peaceful evening, I came to the conclusion that people are just noisy. Think about it. When we eat in a restaurant, music constantly plays. When we get in our cars, we generally turn on the radio. When there is any down time, most of us pull out the smart phones or plug in our ear buds. Heck, we don't even like our trucks to be quiet – we have to put on pipes to beef up the sound of our exhaust.

In general we do not like silence because, in my opinion, silence makes us uncomfortable. I believe there are several reasons for this, but the biggest is the removal of distractions. In silence we are forced to be alone with our thoughts or the lack thereof. We don't like to be quiet because we don't like to think. Consider the word "amused" which comes from "a" which means "no" and "muse" which means "think". Put them together and you have "no think".

We all know Americans like to be amused. But that's not God's way. He tells us through the psalmist that we are to be still and know who He is. Another translation says to quit striving or to be quiet. It is in those times of quiet that we begin to understand something of the personhood of our Lord because our attention is on Him.

It's like this. If you ever have had a large flock of ducks hit your decoys, you know you have to pick one quacker to shoot if you are going to put any meat on the table. If you just sling your shotgun to your shoulder and start flinging steel, you will miss every time. Believe me, I know because I've done both. When you block out all other distractions, you are able to focus on that which is important.

So the next time you are tempted to pop in the ear buds or binge watch Netflix, step back and take a time out from the noise. You might be surprised at what you'll hear.

Do you consistently have times that are "quiet"? What are a few ways these could help you?

Week 12
The Grace of a Grandpa

Grandpa and me

Proverbs 25:11 A word fitly spoken is like apples of gold in a setting of silver.

My Grandpa Worrell was a lot of things: a railroad man, a bird hunter, a dog trainer, a gardener. But the one thing that sticks out most in my mind was him being patient and kind. I cannot think of a time that I heard him speak a harsh or critical word. And believe me, he had plenty of opportunities to get frustrated when taking a squirrelly, preteen boy hunting and fishing. Take for instance the day he gave me my first pump shotgun.

I remember Grandma and him presenting me with a Remington 870 Wingmaster. I could not wait to try it out, so we called a family friend and asked if we could go to his farm and test-drive it on some rabbits. Up until that time, I had used a single-shot Winchester .410, so that was a major upgrade in my shooting experience.

Grandpa talked me through all of the nuances of using a pump, "Joel this is important. Here is how you slide the shell into the magazine. Here is the release for the action. Here's the safety. Always keep it on until you are ready to shoot. Do you understand? Keep the safety on."

Anxious to get going, I said, "I got it Grandpa. Let's go hunting."

I remember he took the lead as we walked down a weed-choked path trying to kick up some cottontails. I was a couple of yards behind him with a shell in the barrel, loaded just like Grandpa taught me. I was rehearsing in my mind how to pump the forearm after the shot, just like Grandpa taught me. And I had the safety off, which is NOT what Grandpa taught me.

Then it happened. In the semi-hyper state that plagues most early middle school boys, I mindlessly fingered the trigger, the gun went off and a hole appeared in the ground right beside my Grandpa's foot. Time froze with him staring at me holding a smoking gun, mouth agape, wondering if this very large man whose hands were like steel was going to wrap my new shotgun around a tree and then proceed to beat the stupid out of me.

After standing there for several seconds, he walked back to me, took the gun and began again, "Joel, here is the safety. Always keep it on until you are ready to shoot." No hollering. No belittling. I don't even think he said anything to my mother when we returned.

I grew that day in my journey to manhood. I grew in my respect for firearms. I grew in my understanding of responsibility. And I grew in my pursuit of being a man by watching how a godly grandpa taught a grandson with kindness and patience.

How would you describe yourself – patient/wise with words or impatient/harsh with words? Now, how would others describe you? Ask them.

Week 13
The Farmer and the French Press

No regular java for me, thank you

1 Timothy 4:4 For everything created by God is good, and nothing is to be rejected if it is received with thanksgiving.

During a duck hunt on Hog Island, I was sitting around the pot bellied stove in the great room of the lodge talking life with a professor from Southeastern Baptist Theological Seminary and a farmer from eastern Wake Co. As we hit various topics like the Bible, politics, steel shot vs. lead, etc. we somehow started debating how one makes a good cup of coffee.

I thought I was fairly advanced in my percolating prowess in that I liked a particular blend of beans that I ground myself. But as I listened to my professor friend, I found out I was a caveman compared to his prep for the perfect cup. He didn't just grind his coffee beans, he bought a special type of java that he roasted in micro-batches and brewed in a French Press.

As the professor waxed eloquent about the steps he went through in making coffee, my farmer friend who had simply been listening to the exchange asked, "Now let me get this straight; you don't buy Folgers from the store? And you buy green coffee beans from some specialty place that you roast yourself? And then you put them in something called a French Press? Man I don't know about all of that, but I'll tell you one thing – that French Press thing doesn't sound like something a Christian man should get mixed up in." At this last statement, all three of us started howling with laughter.

Fast-forward two months after that conversation. I received a phone call from my farmer friend whose initial statement was, "I have been corrupted!" I was a little taken aback by the force of his statement and asked him what had happened. He replied, "I'm in my shop office sipping a cup of coffee from my new French Press with beans that our professor friend roasted. Ya'll have corrupted me!"

Here's the point. My farming buddy was open to a new experience. I Timothy 4:4 tells believers that all things (not expressly prohibited by Scripture) can be enjoyed because God gives them. So many times we rob ourselves of a blessing because we reject doing something differently or trying something new because we are (a) lazy or (b) afraid or (c) prideful.

So the next time you are tempted to think or say "We've never done it that way before," remember my farmer friend who is probably enjoying a freshly brewed cup of java from his French Press. God gave us all things to enjoy, so boys, go forth and enjoy.

What is your initial response when someone brings a new idea to you? Do you shoot it down, or do you listen and ask questions?

Week 14
Target Practice

Kinsey and me at Deep River Sporting Clays

Rev. 2:4 But I have this against you, that you have abandoned the love you had at first.

One year for Father's Day my daughters gave me a shooting lesson at Deep River Sporting Clays. It honestly was one of the best gifts I've ever received. The instructor walked me through everything from my stance to proper placement of my cheek on the gun's comb. But the best piece of advice he gave me was never to take my eye off the clay.

He said the tendency of most people is to try and aim by finding the bead at the end of the barrel and then attempting to line it up with the target. This may sound right, but it is not because focusing on the wrong thing inevitably leads to a lot of shot hitting nothing but sky. Instead I was told to lock onto the clay first and only then allow my arms to bring the gun up to the shooting position. Don't look away and don't stop moving. When the gun is shouldered, then the trigger is pulled and low and behold, most of the clays end up as dust. What I learned was that the arms automatically go where the eyes are looking, so as long as I keep my vision focused, I will hit more targets than I miss. In fact, I was advised to get rid of any bead on my bird guns because all they do is distract.

Now what does shooting clays have to do with Jesus's words to the Ephesian church in Revelation 2? Just this - they had allowed their vision to be clouded with a lot of other "targets", and they were missing the main thing, Jesus Himself. He commended them for their hard work, faithfulness to right teaching and their endurance. However, there is that small but powerful conjunction that starts verse four, "but". These Jesus followers were going after good things, but in light of loving Christ they were not the best things. In my example, they were looking at the bead at the end of the barrel, they were pulling the trigger, and they were missing because they were looking at the wrong targets. Jesus told them to focus their eyes on Him and then the other issues of life would come into focus.

As Oswald Chambers put it, "Jesus taught that a disciple has to make his relationship to God the dominating concentration of his life and to be carefully careless about everything else in comparison to that."

Week 15
The Deer Whisperer

Philippians 2:3-4 Do nothing from selfish ambition or conceit, but in humility count others more significant than yourselves. Let each of you look not only to his own interests but also to the interests of others.

I'm going to tell you one of my favorite hunting stories of all time. Several years back I took the young son of a good friend deer hunting. The day we picked was a perfect late November afternoon, one of those days when the air is cool, but not cold; the sun is shining, but not too brightly. I just knew we were going to bag a buck.

When I got to my friend's house, his son was jabbering away about this trip. (This kid could flat talk.) He talked non-stop from North Raleigh to the Nash County farm where we were to hunt. He was talking as we got out of the Suburban. He was talking as we were putting on our hunting clothes. He was still talking as we started walking to the stand.

Finally, I asked him if he wanted to see a deer. He enthusiastically responded, "Yes!" To which I replied that the only way we were going to put a buck in the crosshairs was if he could tone down the conversation. He said that was no problem and proceeded to whisper instead of talking. Not what I had in mind, but he was trying.

So now as we made our way to the box stand, he whispered. He whispered as we climbed the ladder. He whispered as we settled into our seats. He never stopped whispering. By this time I was getting a little exasperated because the day was really promising. Our stand was on a small rise overlooking a soybean field that bordered some swampy woods. Food, cover, water, great weather – this was the best day I had seen all season. The conditions were perfect except for the fact that my hunting companion would not stop talking.

I tried one last time, "We are getting in prime time for bucks to come out into this field. Do you want to shoot a deer?"
"Yes sir."
"Alright, give me 45 minutes of silence, and I think we'll have a good chance of pulling the trigger. Do you think you can be quiet for 45 minutes?"
"Yes sir."

"Great."

Twenty seconds later, "Mr. Joel?"

"Yes?"

"When you rotate tires, do you move them front to back or side to side?"

I just started laughing. In fact I was laughing so much I had to put my rifle in the corner of the stand. My young friend had words that just needed to come out, and that was the important thing. It was not about being successful by filling a deer tag. What was important was the opportunity for a man to validate the significance of a boy by putting aside the agenda and simply listening.

What would you have done in this situation? Would taking a deer have trumped listening to a kid? In the final analysis, what is the most important thing?

Week 16
The Declaration of a Duck

Arkansas Greenheads
Look good & taste great

Gen 1:21 So God created the great sea creatures and every living creature that moves, with which the waters swarm, according to their kinds, and every winged bird according to its kind. And God saw that it was good.

During a duck hunt in my home state of Arkansas, one of my North Carolina friends shot his first mallard drake. After retrieving his prize, he turned it over in his hands admiring all of the different colors and said, "Joel, a greenhead is just God showing off." In other words, my well-educated, very successful and highly intelligent friend looked at the beauty of this particular species of waterfowl and had to declare that time plus chance could not produce such complex beauty. A duck became a declaration of God's existence.

Contrast that statement with Frederick Nietzsche's famous statement in 1889, "Whither is God? I will tell you, we have killed him, you and I." His basic premise was that God was an invention of man's imagination. Because we needed to have a way to explain our reason for existence, the thought of a higher power entered the collective mind of humanity. Therefore as man has evolved, he has outgrown the need for God just as one outgrows the belief in Santa. What we have is a battle between two worldviews. Naturalism says that the forces of nature adequately explain everything while theism begins with God as the source of all things.

Since Genesis is the foundational book of the Bible it stands to reason that Genesis 1:1 is a foundational verse.

"In the beginning God..." This is the Hebrew word *Elohim*, which stresses God's majesty and power.

"In the beginning God created..." Created is the word *bara*, used only of the work of God. It is the (no pun intended) genesis of the object, not its manipulation. As men we can make things, but we cannot *bara*. We take things that already exist and combine them into a more complex system, but the act of *bara* is God's work alone.

Genesis 1 not only gives us the basis for our history, but also provides stability for our future. We are not cosmic accidents. Creation is not a freak collision of time and chance. Christianity is not a mental crutch stemming from a biological impulse to explain our reason for being. And a man standing in a flooded Arkansas rice field can see that a mallard declares the creativity of our God.

Week 17
Storm on the Sound

Hurricane Florence vs. a friend's pier and boat lifts on Harkers Island

Matthew 8:26-27 And he said to them, "Why are you afraid, O you of little faith?" Then he rose and rebuked the winds and the sea and there was a great calm. And the men marveled, saying, "What sort of man is this, that even winds and sea obey him?"

Growing up in Arkansas, I duck hunted flooded fields and timber. The most dangerous thing I ever faced was stump jumping cypress knees with a johnboat in the predawn dark on the Bayou DeView. Needless to say when I migrated to North Carolina and had to learn how to hunt coastal big water, I was out of my element. I had no idea about large spreads of decoys or local regs on blind placement. Until my first attempt at hunting the Pamlico Sound, I was ignorant about how fast storms could move in and turn the water from slick as glass to white-capping, boat-swamping waves.

On this particular trip, I was with two other novices. We found a secluded spot, set our spread and then burrowed up in the brush. As we waited on the ducks, we noticed storm clouds beginning to build. The wind picked up to the point we decided it was time to head back to the landing (which incidentally was a long way from where we were sitting).

Suddenly we found out we were in trouble because the storm blew in faster than we could pick up our decoys and ready our boat. It started getting pretty scary as the wind began to howl and lightning began to crash. Finally we were ready to leave, but our little outboard was too small to push the boat and three men with all of their gear across the large expanse of water that was now a boiling cauldron of rolling waves.

And our response to this situation? Prayer. We prayed like our lives depended upon it because they did. Then something happened. The wind stopped roaring, the waves laid down and the lightning stopped. I looked at my boys, they looked at me, and we all said an audible, "Thank you, God!" Then we cranked the motor and scooted across the water to safety.

Prayer is a cry of dependence upon God. I don't believe in the "name it and claim it" theology that says pray the right way and have enough faith and God will grant your requests like some benevolent genie. That is not the purpose of prayer. As C.S. Lewis so wisely put it, prayer changes us, not God.

I hope you don't have to be in a metal boat on open water surrounded by waves that fall in the small craft advisory category before your call on our gracious Lord. We are always dependent upon Him.

When you hear the word prayer, what comes to mind? Is it personal? Is it boring? Is it necessary?

Week 18
Stay With It

Romans 5:3-4 …we rejoice in our sufferings, knowing that suffering produces endurance, and endurance produces character, and character produces hope…

I enjoy taking men duck hunting who have never gone. And I have been blessed by lifelong friends in Arkansas who have allowed me to bring novices to their farms so that they experience the mystique of some of the most famous duck hunting in all of America. The following is about one such time.

In 2001 I had the chance to introduce three of my good friends from North Carolina to Arkansas duck hunting. None of these guys had ever gone after quackers with any seriousness, so to see flocks of hundreds of birds blew them away. Everyone at some point of the three-day hunt got into ducks, everyone except Paul. For some reason he had the worst luck.

I started feeling so bad for him that I went the extra mile to try and put him on some mallards. There was a huge wad of them sitting on one impoundment. I positioned Paul in the place I thought they would fly while I snuck up on them. When I pulled up the ducks flushed, but instead of flying towards my boy, they flew right over me, the exact opposite of what I had planned. So what did I do? I knocked down four while Paul was left twiddling his thumbs. It seemed like he was snakebit; every effort proved futile. If I put him on the right of the group, the ducks came in on the left. If he was in the middle, someone else shot before he did. Even the last day saw bad luck.

We had not pulled the trigger, so when shooting hours went out we unloaded and stepped out of the blind. As soon as we did, six Canadian geese flew 25 feet in front of us, 10 feet off of the ground and in a single-file line. If we had been loaded we could have nailed every one of those honkers. Strike one, two, three, four, five…Paul could not catch a break.

But something funny happened. It didn't matter that his hunting was hard. It didn't matter that he did not have anything to show for all of his effort. He was hooked. So much so that he made the 13 hour drive with me on several more occasions.

My friend's experience illustrates what the apostle Paul wrote regarding the Christian life. It is not readymade, but rather it is a journey with each experience building on the next with the goal of strengthening our faith in Christ. As we pursue Him, even the hard things are used for our good. Suffering infuses steel into our souls, developing in us the ability to endure. And as we endure, we are conformed more to the image of Christ, our ultimate hope.

Duck hunting is not about limits of greenheads every time you hit the water. It is about who you are as an outdoorsman, and every hunt, whether hard or easy, is one more step in your maturation. So it is with following Christ. Stay with it.

Week 19
Sleeping With Snakes

Camp Cordova circa 1985

II Timothy 2:22 So flee youthful passions and pursue righteousness, faith, love and peace…

Every year when we close in on Fall, I begin to reminisce about Camp Cordova. Now for those of you who have never heard of this place (and that would be all of you), it was the name several of my boyhood friends and I gave a farm between Cotton Plant and Hunter, Arkansas where we used to spend the weekends camping and hunting.

Before hunting season ever started, we would take a weekend to prepare the camp for our winter excursions. Butane tanks needed filling, the roads had to be graded, and we had to rid the camper of the rats that had taken up residence during the summer. What I'm about to share with you was a memorable occurrence from one of those September Saturdays.

We spent most of this day working around the campground. It was a little warm for early autumn, so we decided to take a break in the camper after lunch. I opted for a quick nap and headed to my bunk. No sooner had I plopped down on the three-inch foam mattress than I felt something wiggling underneath my head. I jumped up, pulled back the mattress and found that I was sharing my bed with a big, ill tempered cottonmouth who had decided to winter in my bed.

Now what would you have done? Would you have placed the mattress back over the snake and laid down to resume your rest? Would you have tried to reason with him saying that he really didn't belong in your bunk; his place was outside in the woods among the other forest creatures? Or would you have done what I did? RUN!

Why do I tell you this story? Because too many times we are apt to coexist with sin instead of fleeing from it. While we wouldn't think twice about giving a wide berth to a venomous snake, in everyday life we sometimes tolerate that which is just as deadly to our souls.

In II Timothy 2:22, Paul doesn't say, "Find a way to coexist with sin." The picture he paints here is vivid and cannot be interpreted any other way than to do an about face and run in the opposite direction when confronted with sin.

I don't think anyone would say that I was overreacting by sprinting out the door and away from danger. So why in the world are we afraid of appearing fanatical when it comes to holiness?

Let's not tolerate snakes in the bed.

Week 20
Shooting Hours and Sirens

Proverbs 28:1 The wicked flee when no one pursues, but the righteous are bold as a lion.

The statue of limitations has expired, so I feel safe telling this story. I obey state and federal game laws. Period. I don't spotlight deer. I don't fudge when it comes to shooting hours. On those rare occasions when I catch a lot of fish, I keep my limit. In other words, I follow the rules. But I was not always ironclad in my resolve when it came to following hunting and fishing regs.

I was 16 and duck hunting by myself on the backside of a friend's farm. I had not had much luck that afternoon, but as the daylight faded and shooting hours passed, dozens of wood ducks began hitting the water where I was sitting in my johnboat. At first I just enjoyed the sight, but then the temptation became too great, and I pulled down on an unsuspecting drake as he cupped on my decs.

The gun went off, the duck went down, and all of a sudden a siren began wailing. Busted by the law! I was scared out of my mind. I had pictures racing through my head of being dragged off to jail all on account of one weak moment. So I did what any intelligent teenage boy would do; I hid the duck. Then I hid myself, hoping whatever lawman was waiting for me would get tired and go home. (I never thought about the fact that my vehicle was parked on the road, so all he had to do was run the tags. Intelligent teenage boy is an oxymoron as far as I'm concerned.)

After an hour passed, I slowly paddled out of my hiding place only to find an empty field. No vehicles with blue lights flashing and game wardens with drawn guns. I didn't question why this was. I just got in my ride and tore out to my house as fast I could.

The next day I was at the farm shop of my friend relating what happened. A hired hand heard my story and informed me he was the one who hit the siren. He had been driving by when I popped the bird and thought it would be funny to make me think I had been caught shooting after hours. He really cracked up when he found out I had waited in freezing weather for another solid hour hoping the law had left.

Solomon says the sinner is always afraid of being found out and thus cannot be at peace. It's wearisome and burdensome. Contrast this with what Christ promised when He said He came to provide the abundant life.

Freedom in Christ or fear in my sin, not much of a choice is it?

Week 21
Set the Tone

Daddy's girls

Psalm 73:15 If I had said, "I will speak thus," I would have betrayed the generation of your children.

In *Confessions of a 20th Century Pilgrim,* Malcolm Muggeridge wrote, "For every situation and eventuality there is a parable if you look carefully enough." I could not agree more. God is constantly sending us lessons if we will just look. The following story shows that, as leaders, we set the tone for those who follow.

My twins have always enjoyed fishing, and we've been blessed over the years to have access to some decent holes. When they were around five, we were at a friend's house on Lake Gaston fishing for bream around his dock. I had just bought Kinsey and Kayla their first rod and reels so between baiting hooks, taking fish off of the hooks and dodging hooks, my attention was scattered. Big mistake.

As I was helping Kayla land a fish, Kinsey tied into a fairly large bluegill which was a major fight for her size. During this epic battle, she lost her footing, fell into the water and sank. My reaction was immediate. I jumped in, and with one movement I scooped her out of the water, placed her on the dock and stood in waist deep water holding her while she sat wide-eyed looking at me. No yelling, no crying, no screaming, just resting between Daddy's hands trying to process what happened.

After several seconds, Kinsey blinked and said, "Daddy, I saw fish!" I breathed a sigh of relief. My girl was not scarred for life. She would fish again if my wife would let me take her after hearing I let Kinsey slip overboard.

So how does Ps. 73:15 connect with me standing in four feet of water holding a dripping five-year-old? Those in positions of leadership have a responsibility for setting the tone, especially in the midst of a crisis. My little girl saw her daddy was in control, so she relaxed.

The author of Ps. 73 was Asaph, a leader within the nation of Israel. We don't know what exactly had happened, but he was in the midst of a major struggle. He questioned God about the justice of what he was experiencing, but in verse 15 he said something interesting. Asaph stated that if he had verbalized his struggle it could have damaged those entrusted to his care.

This is not a proof text for emotional stuffing. That is not authentic living. But in our therapeutic crazed society, many people have gone to the other extreme by believing it is their right to emotionally spew.

Asaph showed a better way. He acknowledged that he was struggling, yet he was careful that what he was dealing with did not color how he led the people. Leadership is to be handled with prayerful consideration. Those under our care are looking to us to set the tone.

Week 22
The Poaching Preacher

James 1:14-15 But each person is tempted when he is lured and enticed by his own evil desire. Then desire when it has conceived gives birth to sin, and sin when it is fully grown brings forth death.

When I was growing up, there was a farmer known as Preacher. I have no idea as to whether or not he was a real man of the cloth, but that was what everyone called him. I do know he was a farmer and that his spread was located between Brinkley and Cotton Plant in a place called Dark Corner.

One afternoon during deer season, so the story goes, Preacher had just turned off of the highway and was headed down Dark Corner towards his shop. As he made his way along the gravel road, he looked in the edge of a field and saw a very nice buck standing broadside in the afternoon sun. Preacher looked around and saw no one, so he stopped his truck, jumped out, threw his rifle across the hood and squeezed off a round. Mind you he was driving on a county road and thus was shooting off a county road. That's an offense even in Arkansas.

The deer didn't run, but simply moved his antlered head and flicked his tail. Preacher racked another bullet into the chamber and pulled the trigger only to see his prey still standing with the only movement being his head and tail. Two more shots, two more identical results, and Preacher put his gun down on the hood, raised his hands in the air and waited for the inevitable. He had fallen for a sting operation.

It seems the game warden had heard people were in the habit of shooting deer off this particular road, so he set up his latest toy, a remote controlled deer decoy complete with moving head and tail. When the officers came out to arrest Preacher, he didn't apologize or try to explain his way out of his predicament. He just asked if he could see the grouping of his bullets before they confiscated his gun. It was said he had put a nice tight pattern behind the front shoulder of the decoy, but that was a small consolation seeing that Preacher would never use that firearm again.

Think about the spiral of Preacher's choices. He saw something desirable but outside the boundaries of the law. He looked around to see if anyone was watching, ascertained no one was and proceeded to go hard after the wrong. Sinful desire, when entertained long enough, moves into sinful actions. That's the progression – it begins in the mind way before it becomes reality.

The next time temptation arises, remember Preacher. Sin may promise a trophy but in the end it will only result in loss.

When temptation hits, whatever form it takes, do you have a plan to deal with it?

Week 23
Praying for a Pig

Matthew 4:7, Jesus said to him, "Again it is written, 'You shall not put the Lord your God to the test.'"

The first time I ever went wild pig hunting was on a 2,000-acre plantation in southern Georgia with 15 men from our ministry. When we arrived at the main house, we went in for dinner and then had about 20 minutes of orientation with our hosts. The owner covered basic things like schedule, house rules and gun safety. He ended by talking about what we could and could not shoot and what the consequences were if we shot the wrong thing.

Any hog that was harvested had to be over 150 lbs. It also had to be either a boar or a gilt, a female that did not have piglets. Of course the question arose, how do you know if she doesn't have young? The answer - look at her belly. If it is slick, then pull the trigger. If the pig had, how do I put this…the obvious means of feeding her young hanging from her mid-section, then we had to let her walk. If we shot a momma hog we would be fined $250.00.

I had invited my nephew Tyler to come on this hunt with me. We sat for two days enjoying each other's company but watched nothing but sows and piglets. As our hunt wound down, our trigger fingers began to get itchy. And when your trigger finger gets itchy you start paying more attention to it than your brain.

As we sat in the stand on our last evening, we spotted the black form of a wild pig well over 150 lbs. The problem was it was walking in weeds that obscured the belly so we couldn't see if it was a boar, sow or gilt. My brain told me to pass, but my trigger finger screamed, "Shoot!" Who won the argument? Bang went my .270! The hog rolled over, I high fived my nephew and then asked the big question, "What did I just shoot?"

As I sat in the stand contemplating the fact that I might have shot a $250 piece of pork, I did what most of us do when we are on the edge of a crisis. I prayed. And not just any prayer mind you. I asked God Almighty to make the belly of my pig slick. It sounds just as stupid now as it did when I uttered it.

We got down from the stand, walked the 150 yards where the hog lay, turned it over and there it was, a gilt. And there was much rejoicing.

Now this is not a devo about doing dumb stuff and then asking God to clean it up. Just the opposite. It's about not viewing God as some cosmic janitor whose job it is to pick up after us. He is the Lord and King of the universe, not some spiritual bellboy who is at our beck and call. Prayer, as John Piper says, is the Christ-follower's direct line of communication to the Commander and Chief in this war we call life – not room service in some hotel where we call down to get another pillow for our comfort.

Remember prayer is really about connecting with God Almighty.

Week 24
A Funny Thing Happened On The Way To the Lodge

Michael & Bailey

Prov 26:11 Like a dog that returns to his vomit is a fool who repeats his folly.

My friend Michael Oxner had a chocolate lab named Bailey. She was a sweet family dog but not much help in the duck blind. This is a story about how that dog validated the wisdom of Solomon during an Arkansas duck hunt in 2005.

As we were loading up the truck to head to the lodge, we saw Bailey with her muzzle buried in a pile of rotten deer guts left over from Michael's last kill.

Ox yelled for her to get away, but she could have cared less what her master was saying. She was in scavenger heaven and was not going to be denied her find. Finally Michael had to grab her collar, yank her away from her fetid feast, pick her up and put her in the extended part of his new rig.

We quickly finished loading the rest of our equipment and took off for the lodge. But somewhere between Augusta and Cotton Plant, we heard Bailey making some interesting noises in the back seat. And then it happened… she threw up.

Now Michael has a weak stomach, so this made for a funny scene. When the stench hit him, he started retching. Michael drove with his head out the window yelling at the dog between dry heaves, Bailey kept emptying her stomach, and I howled with laughter.

Ox finally pulled the truck to the side of the road, flung the door open and found that Bailey had not only vomited in his truck but also on his hunting clothes. He started hollering again at the dog between gagging, all the while throwing his hunting apparel in the grass so he could try and clean it. And Bailey's response? She just wagged her tail while trying to get back to the very thing that had just made her sick.

Graphic? Yes, but to the point. There are two types of people in Proverbs – the wise who seek to live life on God's terms and the ones who do things their way with no regard for God or His truth.

Solomon said the latter will keep going back to the very things that make them sick, emotionally, physically, and spiritually, all the while thinking that the putrid offerings of this world are where satisfaction will be found.

We look at a dog's eagerness to eat such offensive things with a mixture of horror and unbelief. Yet Solomon chose a picture that clearly illustrates the offensive nature of our sinful choices. The next time you begin to gravitate towards that which is unholy, remember Bailey.

Are there things that you know are not good for you that you keep going back to? How can you stop? Is there someone who can help you?

Week 25
One Tough Hog

Warthog in Africa

Gen 4:7 ...sin is crouching at the door. Its desire is contrary to you, but you must rule over it.

During my time on this earth, I've had the chance to do some interesting things in the outdoors. Of all of my experiences, the trip to Botswana with my daughters tops them all. In between ministry opportunities and doing a safari where we saw four of the Big Five, I was able to pull down on a nice impala and wart hog.

Now my first stroll through the bush did not have me drawing down on a charging Cape Buffalo with some exotic caliber. But it did afford me an amazing outing in some of the most gorgeous country among some of God's most beautiful animals. Seeing herds of zebra running and spotting kudu in the brush were more than memorable.

The guys I hunted with picked me up at 5:00 a.m., and we drove over an hour towards the South African border. We arrived at a 50,000 acre cattle farm, layered up against the cold, loaded up the 30-06 and began our trek through the brush. Within an hour I had a healthy ring horn impala which we cleaned, skinned and put in the cooler before 10:00 a.m. After lunch my friends decided they wanted to hunt hogs near a watering hole where, incidentally, they had seen a seven foot cobra the past summer.

As we eased along the edge, suddenly the massive shape of a wart hog appeared in front of us. I quickly drew a bead on this African Hogzilla and pulled the trigger. Bam went the 30-06, over rolled the pig, and high-fives were slapped in celebration of another successful stalk.

We waited a few minutes until we felt we had given him enough time to depart this world. And sure enough, when we found him, he seemed to be on his last leg. My 180-grain bullet had done the job.

One of the guys went back for the truck, which left two of us to watch my pig in his death throes. But after about five minutes, his breathing didn't seem to be getting weaker. In fact he seemed to be getting stronger. All of a sudden his eyes popped open, he stood up, backed out of the brush, looked straight at me as if to say nice try, and then he began walking off. I quickly dispossessed him of the notion that he was free to go by putting another bullet in his brain.

When we cleaned him, we were amazed because we saw the damage of my first shot. I had hit his spine cleanly, and a part of the bone ripped apart the upper portion of his heart. A damaged spine and heart, and he still tried to get away!

Now for the application. In Genesis 4, God confronted Cain after he killed his brother Abel. His statement described Cain's sin like an animal waiting in ambush. How true that is. Just when we think we've mastered some thought or behavior, we let our guard down thinking it's over, and what we thought was dead springs up and rips us apart.

Be humble before God and seek His grace and mercy everyday as you put the crosshairs on your sin.

Week 26
Now That's Dedication

Phil 3:13-14 But one thing I do: forgetting what lies behind and straining forward to what lies ahead, I press on toward the goal for the prize of the upward call of God in Christ Jesus.

A friend who writes for a major outdoor publication once told me about an article he did on America's most fanatical deer hunter. I forgot who he said ended up being crowned as the top dog, but if he were to rewrite that piece I would have to insist he bestow the title on my friend Paul.

This particular story took place many deer seasons ago on the property of Paul's family. It was late afternoon when I heard him pull the trigger, followed by what I would describe as a high-pitched war whoop. My first thought was, "He's popped a nice buck and is now making sure I know it." But then I heard another shot and more yelling. I thought, "Man, I wish he'd shut up. He's ruining my hunt with all that racket." Then I heard three more blasts and a loud, "JOEL!" That's when I realized my friend was in trouble.

I unloaded my rifle, scrambled down the ladder and began jogging toward Paul. As I approached his stand and saw him laid out on the ground, I hit a full sprint. When I got to him, he told me he had shot a deer and fallen off the ladder and broken his leg when he got down to claim his prize. To make matters worse, I could see he was going into mild shock.

As I tried to wrap him in my coat to keep him warm, Paul grabbed me and said, "I need you to do one thing before you leave to get help." I thought he was about to say something dramatic like, "Call my wife and tell her I love her."

No, my man who was suffering from a shattered tibia said, "Go over to my deer and count the points." Seriously, he wanted to know how big the rack was! That's dedication; that's being singular in your focus. Nothing and I mean NOTHING was going to deter him from his prize.

That's a redneck application of what the apostle Paul was saying to the Philippians. He wasn't going to allow anything to keep him from his goal of knowing Christ completely. Neither his past as a fanatical persecutor of the church or his present reality of being imprisoned for Christ was going to sidetrack him when it came to following the Lord.

So the next time your spiritual focus gets a little fuzzy, remember if a hunter with a broken leg can be singular in his pursuit of a deer, you can stay locked down on the unchanging character of Christ.

Are there things that keep you from following Jesus? If so, list them out. Now are you willing to ask God to help you overcome these areas of unbelief?

Week 27
Not Much of a Dog

After a long day's hunt

I Cor. 1:26-27 For consider your calling, brothers: not many of you were wise according to worldly standards, not many were powerful, not many were of noble birth. But God chose what is foolish in the world to shame the wise. God chose what is weak in the world to shame the wise.

A while back, one of my daughters went with me to a friend's house so I could review the paperwork for a hunting lease. As we pulled in, Kinsey noticed Robin's duck and bird dogs in the kennel. She looked at me kind of sly like and said, "Don't you wish you had dogs like that daddy?" Here is what she meant by that comment.

Our first dog was Chester, a white, fluffy, effeminate Bichon Frise. (That's French for curly lap dog. Google the breed and try not to laugh.) This canine was the exact opposite of what I wanted. I envisioned a dog that jumped in the water and retrieved ducks. Chester didn't like wet grass. I dreamt of a dog that would ride in the back of my truck. Chester had to ride in the cab with the AC. I wanted a dog that wore a big leather Filson collar. Chester had bows on his ears.

One day I picked our dog up from the groomer and headed home. We were leaving the next morning to visit family in Arkansas, and the girls wanted him to look nice. I have to admit, blown dry and decked out in red ribbons, Chester was something to behold as he looked out the window of my mud-splattered, jacked up Chevy Z71.

As I stopped at the intersection of Creedmoor and Strickland, another truck pulled up on my right, which happened to be Chester's side. The two guys looked at my dog, then at my truck, then at each other, then at me and busted out laughing. It seems a muddy 4x4 and a bow wearing Bichon do not go together in most people's minds. Such a picture is foolish because everyone knows a real hunter is supposed to have a blockheaded lab in the front seat.

Many people respond to the gospel like those two guys did when they saw Chester. They apply conventional wisdom to the human condition and wrongly conclude they have no need for Christ. The gospel makes little sense to the natural mind because it violates our idea of self-sufficiency.

The gospel stands in stark contrast to human wisdom and strength. The words grace and mercy are ego-destroying in that they show the futility of our puny efforts to win God's favor. This is central to Paul's argument. God rescues sinners like us in the most unlikely manner so that redemption is unquestionably of Him. We don't earn it; we just receive it, and that makes as much sense to some people as a sissy dog riding in a manly truck.

Does the gospel make sense to you? What is the gospel? I like Tim Keller's definition, "That we are so sinful that Christ had to die for us, yet we are so loved that He was willing to die for us."

Week 28
Not A Burden

Brothers

Rom 15:1 We who are strong have an obligation to bear with the failings of the weak, and not to please ourselves.

Every January I head back to the motherland for a few days of shooting quackers. I drive by farms that I hunted hard when I was a young man. Today unknown owners have posted them so that I can't set foot on dirt where I once walked, but the memories of those places are as fresh now as they were years ago.

I remember weekends at our so-called deer camp on the Bayou DeView where the food was either undercooked or burned and the camper filthy, but it was heaven for a bunch of teenage boys. I remember shooting my first mallard out of a pit with no top, no duck call, and no decoys – just sheer luck. I also remember bundling up my little brother and carrying him on my back to the blind because he was too small to make the walk by himself.

I'm adopted, but that's never been a big deal to me. I'm grateful to God that He placed me with my mom and dad. However, the Lord is not only a gracious God, but He is also the author of humor. He sprang a good one on my parents when, at the ages of 40 and 42, they had their first natural child, my brother Michael.

There are 13 years between us, and when Mike turned five he started asking to go on some of my duck hunts. This presented a problem, not because I didn't want him to go, but because a lot of the places I hunted were hard to get to. Michael was simply too little to wade to most of my spots. But instead of telling him he couldn't go, I just threw him on my back and hauled him to the blind. I remember hunching over with my 870 in one hand, my blind bag in the other and Michael's little arms wrapped around my neck hanging on for dear life as I walked through thigh-deep water. He never was too heavy, and thank God I was never too busy. Good memories.

It was my privilege and responsibility as his big brother to bring him along. He wanted to be with me, but he was too young to do it on his own. If he was going to go, it was going to cost me something because I was older and stronger. So it is with the church; we have the privilege and the responsibility to help those who may not be as far along in this journey we call the Christian life.

So instead of seeing it as a burden, see it for what it is, a divine privilege. And yes I hunt with my brother when I am in Arkansas, but he's big enough to walk to the blind now.

How do you define leadership? Do you see it as using people to accomplish a goal or developing people while seeking to accomplish a goal?

Week 29
Mallard Machines, Robo Ducks & Death

Prov. 14:12 There is a way that seems right to a man, but its end is the way to death.

It's amazing all of the gadgets that are available to hunters, especially duck hunters. Open up any outdoor catalogue and you are overwhelmed with grown-up boy toys. It used to be old-timers would take a few tame quackers and use them to lure in wild ducks. Decoys of long ago were blocks of wood somewhat shaped and somewhat painted to somewhat resemble a duck. Then we got a little more sophisticated with plastic decs that could be massed produced. And now? Products with names like The Mallard Machine and Robo Duck along with battery powered shakers and decoys that look more realistic than most ducks scream at us to buy, buy, buy so our hunting experiences will be great.

To be honest, I kind of feel sorry for the ducks, but not enough to stop hunting. All they are doing is looking for a place to land, grab a bite to eat and maybe find a girlfriend. Let's look at it from the duck's perspective.

As Mr. Greenhead flies down the Mississippi flyway, he sees a nice flooded rice field which is holding what looks like a couple of dozen of his cousins. He buzzes the field at a high altitude and hears a lot of chattering, even a come back call which makes him drop a little lower. He checks out the action on the water and sees a drake's wings flapping as he gets ready to descend. He also spies a few hens turning butt-up in the water as they dive to find grain. Yes sir, this looks like the place. A place to get his belly filled while making some new friends who are headed south for the winter.

So Mr. Greenhead cups his wings, points his beak into the wind, sets his feet as he gets ready to hit the water, and then he sees four camo'd bubbas and their chocolate lab in a blind that he had thought was a bush. Before he can gain altitude, the steel begins to fly and that closes the last chapter on Mr. Greenhead. Well really the last chapter has him flash fried in bacon grease and served with a peach chutney finishing sauce, but that's not the point.

What he thought was life turned out to be death. What he believed to be for his good ended up with his demise. So it is with us. When we lean on our own understanding and we trust in our limited senses, we are no better than Mr. Greenhead. The world throws things at us on a daily basis that promise peace, joy, satisfaction and purpose. Buy this product; do this set of exercise videos, eat this food; drive this vehicle; land that job…they all point to life, but in the end they all end in the same place.

Are there things that at this moment you believe will bring satisfaction? Have there been past times when you have thought this only to be disappointed? What needs to change?

Week 30
Look Grandpa, I Cleaned Your Gun

1 Pet 1:14-16 As obedient children, do not be conformed to the passions of your former ignorance, but as he who called you is holy, you also be holy in all your conduct, since it is written, 'YOU SHALL BE HOLY, FOR I AM HOLY'.

Whenever I see an older Remington 11-87, I think of the time my friend Michael Oxner literally shaved hundreds of dollars off the value of one of his grandpa's shotguns. Here's what he did.

When Michael was just a wee lad, his granddad won a commemorative 11-87 12 gauge at a Ducks Unlimited banquet. It was a nice piece with gold inlay throughout the metal scrollwork, something you don't see on a normal shotgun. Something that Ox had never seen for sure.

Arque laid the 11-87 on a table and went into another room where he became busy and forgot about the gun. At some point during the evening, Michael strolled through the room and, like any red-blooded boy, was automatically drawn to the shiny 12 gauge like a moth to an open flame. As he looked over the shotgun, he noticed yellow stuff in the fancy etching so he promptly found a toothpick and sewing needle and began tracing the lines in order to remove what he thought was some kind of dirt.

After spending a lot of time at this task, he proudly took the 11-87 to Arque to show him how he had "cleaned" the new gun. Mike's grandpa, a quiet, even-keeled man, took one look at his commemorative shotgun sans the gold inlay and said…well, I can't print what he said, but you get the picture.

Here's the point. Michael took a unique shotgun and turned it into an ordinary 11-87. We do the same thing when we live life on the lesser planes of habit and "have-to" instead of displaying the riches of our gracious Father who, according to the Scriptures, has given us everything.

When people hear the word "holy", they usually have misconstrued ideas of unobtainable spirituality. Nothing could be further from the truth. The word "holy" means unique, set apart. When God says for us to be holy, we must first understand He is stating what has already happened. Through the work of Christ's life, death and resurrection and our faith in Him as Savior and Lord, we are made unique. And it is out of this God-empowered reality that we live our lives so that there is something extraordinary, something that points to His divine work. We don't become holy by doing so many holy acts. Because of Christ we are holy, and thus we simply live out that truth.

So the next time you think holiness is unobtainable, remember God made you to be a trophy that attests to His grace and mercy. And if Ox tries to sell you a DU 11-87, I would pass.

Week 31
Lay Him Down Daddy!

Laid this one down

1 Cor 10:23 'All things are lawful', but not all things are helpful. 'All things are lawful', but not all things build up.

As I was flipping through the pages of one of my hunting and fishing photo albums, I came across a picture of Kinsey at age nine with a .243 on her shoulder and a lollipop in her mouth. It was a reminder of a hunt that took place years ago on a friend's farm outside of Scotland Neck.

My friend managed for trophy bucks, but he told us that Kinsey could take whatever she wanted. As we sat in the box stand and watched the sun set behind the tree line, a young buck walked out and began feeding in the food plot directly in front of us.

His body wasn't big, and his antlers had no size, but that didn't seem to matter to Kinsey. She whispered, "Let's shoot him Daddy." I whispered back, "No, he's too small." She kind of bowed up and whispered a little more emphatically, "Let's shoot him Daddy! Mr. Johnson said we could!" I told her again that we were going to let this one walk. That's when my little nine-year-old girl looked at me and said, "Daddy, lay him down!"

After I quit laughing, I explained that we didn't shoot something just because we could. I told her that the buck was young and needed to grow. I tried to help her understand that even though Mr. Johnson had given us permission to take whatever came our way, we needed to consider what was best for him and his farm. I don't know if I convinced her that it was right to let the deer walk, but she submitted by chomping down on her sucker in frustration and watching the deer through her scope.

Here's the application. Just because we can do something does not necessarily mean we should. Kinsey's struggle with not shooting a small deer even though she had permission illustrates this key principle in the Christian life.

Paul was dealing with a fractured Corinthian church; one of its main problems was people demanding their own way. That is the death knell for any human effort: a church, business or marriage. Once we begin waving the banner of our rights in the faces of those around us we've lost the battle. We may have right on our side. We may even have "permission" from the Scriptures to do a certain thing. But as Paul states in the next verse, that is not the greater good. The greater gospel-adorning good is to seek to bless our neighbors.

So the next time you have the "right" to do something, step back and make sure that by exercising it you do not give offense to the cause of Christ. Even if we have permission to "lay him down", it's sometimes better to let the little bucks walk.

Week 32
Kayla and the Copperhead

Kayla and I at a Phi Mu father/daughter event

Deut. 6:6-7 And these words that I command you today shall be on your heart. You shall teach them diligently to your children, and shall talk of them when you sit in your house, and when you walk by the way, and when you lie down, and when your rise.

Since Kimberly's family is from the western part of the state, we've spent years exploring that area of North Carolina. One of the traditions we've developed is taking the girls to what we call "The Rocks". This is a section of roaring whitewater right off of the road that leads to Highlands. The stream is strewn with boulders and has a stone ledge that's about 20 feet above a very deep pool where people can jump. The girls have made this one of their favorite playgrounds, so it didn't surprise me when one Fourth of July they asked me to drive them to "The Rocks".

When we arrived, Kinsey headed to the ledge ready to hurl herself into space and drop two stories into the pool of cold water below. For some reason Kayla didn't want to engage in this time-honored practice, so she took off downstream climbing the boulders. As a middle-aged man, I decided my best place was a sunny spot where I could soak up the warmth and keep an eye on both of my daughters.

I had not been settled very long when I noticed Kayla headed back towards me. When she got to my spot she told me she almost put her hand near a copperhead that was sunning itself in a crevice. I asked her to describe what she saw and, sure enough, what she said matched up with this member of the pit viper family. I was proud that she handled the situation just like I taught her years ago.

Ever since they could walk, the girls have joined me in some of my outdoor adventures. They've sat in the flooded fields of Arkansas waiting on mallards. They've hunkered down in box stands looking for deer in eastern North Carolina. Kimberly has even let them go wild boar hunting with me in southern Georgia. And because we've spent so much time outside, I've instructed Kayla and Kinsey about what to do when they came across a snake. I remember them being around five-years-old and telling them to walk along until I said snake. They were to then freeze, look around, spot the animal and slowly back away. And that's exactly what Kayla did. She didn't panic, scream or run. She simply stopped and quietly went in a different direction so as to not startle the snake and risk a strike.

So it is with our children when it comes to this world. "Serpents" abound. As parents, it is our responsibility and privilege to train them according to God's truth in how they should handle potential dangers. The church, although important in the spiritual growth of our kids, is not the main means of discipleship. Parents have been tapped by God to open the eyes of their children to His love. Dads, help your kids know how to deal with the "copperheads" in life.

Week 33
It's Who You Know...

Ox and I after a day of chasing ducks

I John 2:1 ...we have an advocate with the Father, Jesus Christ the righteous.

Over the years Ox has provided some of the best duck hunting opportunities when I have come in with my friends from North Carolina. One year he outdid himself by not only giving us access to his farms but also to an exclusive duck lease where he was a member.

It was epic. Feathers literally filled the sky. We had flight after flight coming into our spread. It was one of those hunts where we could not do anything wrong. The ducks simply wanted in that field.

The last day we were in Arkansas, Michael called me and said that he was not going to be able to meet us due to some other responsibilities. But we were cleared to go back to the lease and hunt Friday afternoon. My response - no way. He was our ticket to the property, and I was not stepping on that farm without him. He told me there was absolutely nothing to worry about. He had talked with all the club members; no one was hunting until Saturday, so we were free to hit the honey hole one more time. Ox finally convinced me that everything was good. It was not.

Less than five minutes after we set up, a truck stopped on the road, a man began walking towards us, and he did not look happy. Busted...I knew this was going to happen. I told my guys to hang tight while I went out and tried to clear up the problem. I thought I was just going out to meet a disgruntled club member who wanted to throw his weight around. Imagine my surprise when I saw the badge on his chest, the 9mm in his holster and the citation book in his hand. This wasn't some yahoo wanting to chew us out for hunting on his lease. This was the law coming to arrest us for trespassing.

What was interesting was as soon as I mentioned the name of Michael Oxner, everything was golden. The officer knew Michael, put up his ticket book, and he and I stood in thigh-deep water surrounded by duckweed and shot the breeze. We even pulled a prank on Ox by texting him that I had been arrested and he needed to bring bail money to the jail in Augusta.

My association with Ox was all I needed. I had no authority on my own to be hunting that property. But because of who I knew, the law became my friend, not my enemy. So it is with Christ. The enemy comes and says we are guilty; we have broken the law; we stand condemned. And he would be right if the story ended with us. However, it doesn't. Christ came into the world to save sinners (I Tim. 1:15); He who knew no sin took on our sin so that we might become the righteousness of God in Him (II Cor. 5:21). It's Who you know that makes the difference. Without Him, we are guilty. But thanks to God we have an Advocate who is greater than the law.

Week 34
Behind the Veil

Kinsey with Dixie ducks

Heb. 10:19-20, 22 Therefore, brothers, since we have confidence to enter the holy places by the blood of Jesus, by the new and living way that he opened for us through the curtain, that is, through his flesh...let us draw near with a true heart in full assurance of faith.

One duck season, my daughter Kinsey had the chance to accompany me to a very special hunting spot that my good friend Ox owns. He and his brother Willie have several hundred acres that border a federal wildlife refuge which holds tens of thousands of ducks every year. Since the property is landlocked, the feds have to give Michael a right away through the sanctuary. It is a unique experience to drive up to the large metal gate marked with a sign that says "Area Closed" and a chain with a huge brass lock stamped with the initials of the U.S. Federal Wildlife Department, pull out a key, open the lock and drive through the gate.

On this day Kinsey and I loaded up in the Man Machine (aka the camo Burb), and drove to the shop at Dixie Farms where we met Ox. We threw our stuff in his truck, headed down the road through the gate to the backside of the farm for an afternoon of hunting. After our shoot we were standing at Mike's rig watching the setting sun when we saw an incredible sight. All of a sudden the evening sky was full of ducks headed back to the refuge to roost. I'm not talking about a few healthy flocks. It was one solid cloud of mallards, pintails, gadwalls, widgeons, spoonbills and ringnecks. There were so many you could not see the beginning and the end at the same time. It was a massive flight of feathers which almost blotted out the sky for a few minutes.

As we sat on Mike's truck watching this sight, I told Kinsey that she was witnessing something few people living today have ever seen. I wanted her to soak up this experience and to understand what a privilege it was to be on the backside of Dixie looking and listening to thousands of ducks in the air above us. And it was all because she was with the one who could drive through the gate.

And so it is with God. Consider what Christ's life, death and resurrection have accomplished for us. It is because of Him that our sin is obliterated. It is because of Him that Heaven is thrown open to us. It is because of Him that we enter the presence of our God as His sons. It is because of Him that we trade the trinkets of this passing world for that which is eternal.

It's amazing what you'll see when you are with the one who can open the gate.

Week 35
How Not to Get a Camo Burb or a New Four-Wheeler

The big reveal

Prov. 31:10-12 An excellent wife, who can find? She is far more precious than jewels. The heart of her husband trusts in her, and he will have no lack of gain. She does him good, and not harm, all the days of her life.

My mid-life crisis has come and gone. Instead of a little red sports car or hair plugs, I camo'd my '99 Chevy Suburban old school style. I thought the paint job turned out kind of nice. In fact, most people seemed to like it, except the pseudo-chic gals that haunted a particular Raleigh mall. I used to love picking my daughters up from that den of materialism in my urban assault vehicle and watching Barbie wannabes gasp in horror as I rumbled by.

However, the problem with my Burb's new look was my bride didn't know it was coming. Well technically she had given me a blessing of sorts. When I first floated the idea of painting it various shades of green and brown she kind of smiled and nodded her head. That's all the approval I needed.

This approach was employed by another friend of mine when he wanted to get a 4-wheeler.

When he was a newly married husband, he really wanted an ATV, which any outdoorsman knows falls more into the category of necessity than preference. So how did he go about asking his wife? He waited until she was pregnant with their first child and was suffering through a very intense time of morning sickness before he broached the subject. And if I remember correctly, he sprung the question of making this purchase one Saturday morning while she was recovering in the bed after an all night battle with nausea.

I think the conversation went something like, "Hey Sweetie, can I get a new 4-wheeler?" To which she replied, "Ughhhhhh." She didn't say no, due to the fact that she simply couldn't say anything. So off my boy goes and buys a new Arctic Cat.

Don't do what we did. First of all you are not assured of your bride's reaction. My friend and I were blessed. My wife stood in silence for about 10 seconds staring at this manly monstrosity now sitting in her driveway. She then looked at me and said, "Honey, take me for a ride." And there was much rejoicing. My friend's wife, after many years of a sweet marriage that has produced three great kids, laughs at how her hubby scored his ATV. In fact she's the one who told me this story.

Second, when God gives a wife, she is to be treated as the treasure she is. Proverbs says she is worth more to her husband than any earthly fortune he could ever amass. So take it from two reformed rednecks – let your wife pick the color of the camo and the make of the 4-wheeler.

Week 36
Her Best Day Ever

A young Kayla with our buck

**Psalm 127:3-5 Behold, children are a heritage from the LORD…
Like arrows in the hand of a warrior are the children of one's
youth. Blessed is the man who fills his quiver with them!**

Kayla was around eight years old when this particular story occurred.
We arrived at a friend's farm around 3:00 p.m. and walked to a big
open box stand that had a commanding 300 yard view. We sat and
talked while Kayla popped candy in her mouth from the "survival
provisions" I had packed. As the sun began setting, I handed her the
binoculars and told her to start looking because the deer were about
to move.

After 10 minutes of her glassing the lanes, she said, "Daddy, a
deer is coming our way. It looks like a buck." I took a peek through
the lenses; sure enough, a nice seven pointer was walking towards us.
As I started getting my rifle in position, Kayla said, "You aren't going
to shoot him are you Daddy?" I replied yes which promptly launched
a whispering argument with her telling me not to shoot and me
emphatically stating that I was going to squeeze the trigger. (Side note
– my girl was not trying to save the deer. She has sensitive ears and
simply didn't want to hear the noise of the rifle. Now before you say
she should have been wearing ear protection, she was.)

As the deer came closer, I told Kayla in no uncertain terms that I
was taking the shot. As soon as I pulled the trigger, the buck jumped,
spun around and took off running. And the girl who seconds ago was

telling me not to shoot looked at me and yelled, "How could you miss that deer?" I laughed and said that I had not missed and that it was time to go find our trophy.

We walked about 40 yards into the woods and there he lay. As soon as Kayla saw him, she started jumping up and down cheering, "We got our deer!" And when I told her we were getting a four-wheeler from my friend's barn to haul in our buck, her enthusiasm went to a whole other level. After loading up the deer and then Kayla on the ATV, she looked at me and said, "Daddy, this is my best day ever."

Many seasons have come and gone since that day, and Kayla has grown to a point that she no longer wants to go hunting with her father. But the memories of that day will be with me for as long as I live. Children are truly a gift from God; take every opportunity to enjoy them.

Week 37
Growing Gray Together

Ox, Trey and I on our annual Arkansas duck hunt

Prov 20:29 The glory of young men is their strength, but the splendor of old men is their gray hair.

My relationships with Michael Oxner and Trey Clifton have spanned over 40 years. I became friends with Trey around age five when our moms made what is now known as a play date. I hate that phrase. My friendship with Ox began with a fight on the fifth grade playground after I thought he was cheating in box ball. It wasn't much of a fight, but it was bad enough that we were sent to the principal's office. We decided while sitting in the hallway we were not mad at each other, so we just walked out of the office and never argued again.

The three of us have buried tractors, ATVs and family vehicles while seeing how far we could drive through muddy fields. Together we've chased deer, shot ducks, gigged frogs and fished. In other words, we've grown up and subsequently grown gray together.

Now I'm not saying we're elderly, but when I see pictures from years gone by, and I look at us now we do look more mature. Laugh lines have replaced pimples; six pack abs have rounded out just a bit, and blond hair has started to get a little whiter and a little thinner.

As a culture we spend a lot of time and effort trying to stay young.

We hold up the 20 and 30 somethings as the holy grail of existence. You know what? I'm good with the aging process as long as I have godly men who make the journey with me. Michael and Trey are a few guys with whom God has given me the privilege of growing gray. I hope you can say the same.

Who are the men making this journey with you? How are you being intentional with spending time together?

Week 38
Frog Catching and Cotton Mouths

Agkistrodon piscivorus aka cottonmouth

2 Cor. 11:3 But I am afraid…your thoughts will be led astray from a sincere and pure devotion to Christ.

Most people who have grown up in the rural South have experienced the time honored tradition of frog gigging, which is how one obtains the delicacy known as frog legs. If you're not familiar with gigging, here's what you do. You get your buddies together, grab a light and start shining ditch banks or backwater bayous for the telltale sign of two eyes peeping out of the water. When you see a frog staring back at you, hold the light on him to freeze the frog in place while someone with the gig, a large bamboo pole with a small trident spear attached to the end, slips up quietly and jabs him. Well this particular story is about the evening some running buddies and I decided we were going to be more sporting by leaving the gig and attempting to catch the frogs with our hands.

Michael, our friend Ray and I piled in a pickup and headed to a farm to try our experiment. Ox was driving, I was shining, and Ray was in the back waiting to jump in the water and catch the frogs. We had a measure of success that evening, so when the light hit a pair of eyes just above the water, we stopped and Ray eased into the water to catch what looked like a big bullfrog. He reached down and made a perfect grab, but it was not a frog – it was a cottonmouth, also known as a moccasin, one of the most poisonous snakes in the Delta.

When Ray came up with it, he looked at the white mouth unhinged, fangs extended, let out a scream, cocked his arm back and flung that moccasin as far as he could – the thing looked like a scaly propeller flying through the air. At that moment our noble idea of being more sporting when it came to our quest for frog legs died. We went back to the 10-foot pole.

Here's the point. Paul was dealing with people who were being tricked into believing another "gospel". False teachers had infiltrated the Corinthian church and were undermining biblical truth. And the sad fact was that some believed the lies and walked away from the simple calling to love Christ completely. They had heard the gospel, but then allowed themselves to be seduced by something that kind of looked like the truth but was in reality heretical. And instead of chunking it (like Ray with the moccasin) they held onto it to their detriment.

We live in a world today that says all religions are the same. Don't buy the lie because such a belief make as much sense as saying a cottonmouth is the same as a bullfrog.

Week 39
Final Exam

1 Cor. 3:11-13 For no one can lay a foundation other than that which is laid, which is Jesus Christ. Now if anyone builds on the foundation with gold, silver, precious stones, wood, hay, straw, each one's work will become manifest, for the day will disclose it, because it will be revealed by fire, and the fire itself will test what sort of work each one has done.

Many years ago when Kimberly and I moved to Fort Worth, Texas, I learned a hard lesson about the temporal nature of this life. We lived in a rough part of the city, so I took one pump shotgun for protection. I left all of my other firearms at my parent's house thinking they were safer in a small town than in a big city.

One morning I received a call from my parents informing me that there had been a break-in at their home, and the thieves had cleaned out my gun cabinet. To say I was devastated would be an understatement. Although my shotguns and rifles were not worth a lot of money, they had stories attached to them, so the emotional tie was much greater than any dollar amount. These people didn't take pieces of metal and wood; they took physical connections to my past. But as I wrestled with my feelings, I was reminded that nothing in this world is forever. Eventually everything but my relationship with Christ will be gone.

Paul understood this better than most people. He was educated, powerful and influential - qualities so many people pursue. Yet when Christ rescued him from his sin, Paul began to understand that outside of Christ nothing would last. In fact, he painted a pretty vivid picture in his letter to the Corinthian church of two believers; both were saved by faith, but one pursued Christ while the second went after other things. Not bad things, but rather things that he desired and did in his own power.

Paul said both men would stand before the Righteous Judge and have their lives tested. The foundation is Christ, and that cannot be destroyed. But notice what will happen to the things they have given themselves to. One man's life will withstand the test and therefore have eternal significance. The other will have everything he considers important literally burned up, and a lifetime of achievements will turn to ashes.

We have two simple questions in front of us. First, have we submitted to the lordship of Christ in our lives, trusting in Him for the forgiveness of our sin and then accepting His righteousness as our own? If so, how are we living out the reality of the gospel? We will stand before God and have our lives judged, not with regards to our salvation, but rather for how we allowed the gospel to impact our lives. In other words, He will not ask us if we accepted Christ but what we did with Christ. And that puts the things of this world (gun collections included) into perspective.

Week 40
Effective But Not Legal

Trey and I with a legal catch circa 1984
No explosives were used to take these fish

Prov 28:20 A faithful man will abound with blessings, but whoever hastens to be rich will not go unpunished.

Due to the questionable nature of the following story, some of the names have been changed to protect the guilty. Most of us have heard stories or jokes about guys who have used dynamite to fish. I've seen this tactic in real life. Since this activity is highly illegal, and I have no idea as to whether the statute of limitations apply, I will call my friend who utilized this method Horatio. I've personally never known anyone by that name so forgive me if that happens to be yours.

I recall meeting several of my high school running buddies on the backside of Horatio's farm one evening. We were supposed to run trotlines, but Horatio had other ideas. He produced several sticks of explosives which were generally used to blow up beaver dams so the water didn't back up into the fields and flood the crops. I asked, "Horatio, what are you going to do with that dynamite?" Horatio replied, "I'm going fishing." He proceeded to cut the fuses, crimp the blasting caps, strike the match, hurl the burning stick into the bar ditch and run.

One minute went by with all of us standing a hundred yards back with our fingers in our ears when, kaboom, water went straight up in the air just like a depth charge explosion on a WWII movie. We raced to the waters edge to see what Horatio's fishing experiment produced, and there they were. Fish by the dozens floating on their sides just waiting to be scooped up. No long hours of baiting hooks or fighting mosquitoes or coming back sunburned…just light the fuse, run, and fill your cooler. Just for the record, the fish we (I mean Horatio) did not take home revived and swam off. It seems the explosion stunned them but didn't have much killing power. Dynamite proved to be an effective but not exactly legal or safe fishing method.

Here's the application. Just because something is effective or even efficient does not mean we should automatically do it. A life based solely on these goals misses the benchmark for the godly man. Solomon says the faithful person receives the blessing. In other words, production or results are not the focus. Simply living life on God's terms and trusting Him are the goals. We are called to holiness and to live lives that demand a supernatural explanation, not practices that produce some desired result. I've seen too many people looking for the shortcut in life that will provide the biggest bang. The problem with focusing on "the bang" is that it can blow up on you.

Week 41
Dry-Rotted Waders and White Washed Graves

Kinsey in the blind on Cypress Slough

Matthew 23:27-28 "For you are like whitewashed tombs, which outwardly appear beautiful, but within are full of dead people's bones and all uncleanness. So you also outwardly appear righteous to others, but within you are full of hypocrisy and lawlessness."

Once when my family was visiting my parents, Kinsey asked if she could go duck hunting with Ox and me. Of course I said yes, and I knew Michael would not mind at all if she came. The problem was that Kinz didn't have any waders, and where we were hunting required more than knee boots.

I asked my parents if they had any ideas, and they suggested a family friend who had raised five daughters to duck hunt. So I called Sam, and he had a set. The only issue was that he could not vouch for their ability to keep the water out. It seems the last time they were used had been several years before. He felt they would be alright, but no guarantees.

I drove out to Sam's house with Kinz. He brought out the boots. They looked pretty decent. My biggest concern was all of the spiders that I shook out. We thanked Sam and headed back to my parents where I proceeded to wash and clean the waders before our afternoon hunt.

We checked them out pretty thoroughly. Kinsey put them on, and they fit. I sprayed her down with the water hose to see if she could feel any leaks. She didn't. So we loaded up in the Suburban and headed to Dixie.

We met Michael and drove to the flooded field where we had just been laying out the mallards. I was really excited for my daughter to see what duck hunting could be like. But that experience never happened because within 30 seconds of Kinsey stepping into the water, she found that the waders had not just one leak but multiple points of entry for the water. She was soaked. The hunt was over.

In Matthew 23, Jesus is dealing with the scribes and Pharisees, two groups of religious leaders who looked like they had it together from the outside. They knew the Law. They followed it to the letter. They made a big show of how they lived according to the scriptures. But Christ nailed them by comparing them to graves that had been painted pretty on the outside but were full of decay and rotting corpses. You see the issue was not what they did, but who they really were.

Anyone can act like they are righteous for a certain amount of time, but eventually what is on the inside comes out. Or in Kinz's case, what was on the outside came in eventually. Either way our call is to be authentic men who pursue God wholeheartedly, and thus we will not be dry-rotted waders or whitewashed tombs.

Week 42
Deer in the Dark

Prov. 4:18, But the path of the righteous is like the light of dawn, which shines brighter and brighter until full day.

I love being in the woods or on the water before the sun comes up. It is one of those small blessings of life to see the world waking up. But one of the drawbacks to being on the deer stand before dawn is the fact that in the dim light everything looks like a deer. And I mean everything.

Any deer hunter has had the following experience. You look to your left and see a buck's antlers sticking out from behind a tree. As you stare down the shooting lane on your right, you swear you see a big doe emerge. Behind you in the thick brush you make out the grey coat of a deer bedded down from last night. And as you gaze at these you are sure that you see movement. You slowly get your weapon safely positioned so that when it gets light you'll be ready. Your heart is racing at the thought of filling three of your tags in one morning.

Then the sun comes up, and everything is revealed for what it truly is. The buck's antlers are nothing but a low gnarled branch on a jack pine. The doe at the end of the shooting lane is a bush. The bedded down deer in the thick stuff is simply a discolored path of vegetation. Strikes one, two and three. Put the .270 back in the corner of the stand, pour a cup of coffee and try to calm your nerves.

Solomon tells us this is basically life. Those who desire to live on God's terms will have their lives illuminated by His truth so that things take on their true forms. The work of our hands is no longer about a paycheck but is seen as an opportunity to represent Christ. Our wives are not roommates, but are women to cherish, love and protect. Our children's interruptions are not burdensome but blessings. Even painful things are seen in a different light.

Why is this? Because the Source of all truth is leading. Jesus is not an insurance policy or a good luck charm. He is the Light of the world and in Him is no darkness. In Jesus we see life for what it is – a glorious adventure meant to be lived on His terms.

Just as we wait for the sun so that we know what we're aiming for, so we wait for the Son to show us what life is about. If you don't, you'll waste your time staring at nothing but a branch of a jack pine.

Week 43
Close Doesn't Count

Wet but successful

Matthew 7:13-14 Enter by the narrow gate; for the gate is wide and the way is easy that leads to destruction, and those who enter by it are many. For the gate is narrow and the way is hard that leads to life, and those who find it are few.

One duck season, I had a unique opportunity in to hunt tundra swan in Hyde Co. with two friends. I was treated to outstanding food (oysters, grilled chicken, chocolate chess pie, etc.), comfortable accommodations within walking distance of famed Lake Mattamuskeet and incredible shooting (see photo above). My host went out of his way to make sure this outing was memorable.

On the morning of the hunt, I was driven to the levy where our pit was located. After giving us instructions about turning on the pump and how to place the spread, my host left to park the truck. Since Tedd and I had our marching orders, we headed to the pit, grabbed a couple of dozen decs and started into the field. When I stepped into what I thought was knee-deep water, I found myself up to my armpits with it pouring over the top of my waders. I quickly did a little panic induced breaststroke and got back on dry ground safe but soaked.

As I tried to regain a little composure after my surprise dunking, I looked to my left. In the predawn light, I saw two wooden survey stakes in front of our pit. I deduced that they held some importance and yelled, "TC, I think we're supposed to walk between those stobs." And I was right. The stakes marked a 10 foot wide path that was covered with only shin-deep water which allowed Tedd to breeze over the bar ditch nice and dry. There was only one way to enter the impoundment, and any other effort resulted in wet waders.

Many in our culture believe Jesus to be a good teacher, maybe even an example to imitate. But He never left His identity in doubt. His words in Matthew's account are hard and harsh, but truth sometimes is both. There is exclusiveness to His teaching; Jesus says He is THE way to the Father and eternal life and yet few find Him. Why? It is because Christ demands everything. Not a few hours on Sunday or a couple of dollars for the plate or a perfunctory prayer over a meal. No God, as Bonheoffer said, bids us come and die in order to find life. And the only way to life is through the Son, period.

So learn from my example; when the path is clearly marked, take it. You'll arrive safely on the other side and, in my case, dry.

Week 44
Change Your Tactics

Acts 17:16, 22-23 Now while Paul was waiting for them at Athens, his spirit was provoked within him as he saw that the city was full of idols…So Paul, standing in the midst of the Areopagus said: "Men of Athens, I perceive that in every way you are very religious. For as I passed along and observed the objects of your worship, I found also an altar with this inscription, 'To the unknown god.' What therefore you worship as unknown, this I proclaim to you."

As outdoorsmen we have to adapt to weather conditions, different geography and varied species of fish and fowl. If you want to ensure an empty cooler, just keep doing the same thing over and over with no thought as to whether it is producing solid results.

A couple of years ago I was hunting with Ox. It had been a good morning with steady flights of greenheads hitting our decoys. While we hunted we heard some guy just showering down on his duck call. He was throwing the book at the birds. Highballs and comeback calls were blaring. I guess he thought loud was the key, but he never squeezed off a shot. Why? Because he didn't take into consideration that by the time the quackers have hit Arkansas, they have heard about every call, seen every spread with shakers and mojos and been shot at all the way down the Mississippi. That means you have to hunt smart because the birds have become very cagey. Not this dude, his calling was loud, long and ultimately lonely. No shot, no ducks.

Now consider how you share Jesus. Evangelism is not done just one way. You have to be open to different tactics as God leads. Look at Paul.

In Acts 17 he was surrounded by the idols of a pagan society and it troubled him. Yet he did not blast them for their heretical beliefs. He took what they knew (idol worship) and used it to make a beeline to the cross. He considered who he was talking to and where he was. Then he adjusted his presentation of the truth. Notice I said "presentation". Paul never adjusted the truth, but he was flexible in what method he used to share Jesus.

Never back down from the truth, but be wise in how you present it.

Week 45
I'm Thankful For...

James 1:17 Every good gift and every perfect gift is from above, coming down from the Father of lights with whom there is no variation or shadow due to change.

- I am thankful to hear whistling wings in the predawn darkness of an Arkansas duck hunt.
- I am thankful for eyes to see a buck chasing a doe in the middle of rut.
- I'm thankful for old friends who have hit the water and the woods with me for over 40 years.
- I'm thankful for a grandpa who took the time to teach me how to shoot and fish.
- I'm thankful for a dad who didn't know anything about the outdoors yet took his five-year-old son deer hunting at the Fuller Deer Camp.
- I'm thankful for a wife who gives me time in the deer stand and the duck blind and on the boat.
- I'm thankful for daughters who spend time with me in the stand and on the boat.
- I'm thankful for a family who enjoys grilled venison kabobs and flash fried duck breast.
- I'm thankful for a friend who shares his recipes for making said kabobs and duck breast.
- I'm thankful for the smell of freshly ground and brewed coffee on a cold January morning.
- I'm thankful for the beauty of a full moon rising over Core Banks while I sit in a stake blind.
- I'm thankful for tight lines while fishing for red drum on Shark Island.
- I'm thankful I saw the sunrise in the hill country of Botswana, Africa while glassing for impala.
- I'm thankful for a full gun safe.
- I'm thankful I can buy ammo by the case.
- I'm thankful for flushing coveys.

- I'm thankful for gobbling toms at dawn.
- I'm thankful for a mom and dad who adopted me and gave me a place to belong.
- I'm thankful for in-laws who love me as their own son.
- I'm thankful for nephews who believe their Juncle a.k.a. Uncle Jojo is a great outdoorsman despite evidence to the contrary.
- I'm thankful for memories of running trotlines with boyhood buddies.
- I'm thankful that Christ Jesus came into the world to save sinners, of whom I am chief.
- I'm thankful that nothing can separate me from the love of Christ.
- I'm thankful that God in His sovereign will chose me before the foundation of the world.
- I'm thankful that my sins are cast as far as the east is from the west.
- I'm thankful that Christ bore my guilt, paid my debt and gave me His righteousness.
- I'm thankful that I have a copy of God's truth.
- I'm thankful for the church.
- I'm thankful that I have freedom in Christ.
- I'm just thankful.

Week 46
Be Prepared

A few ducks from Core Sound

I Peter 3:15, But in your hearts honor Christ the Lord as holy, always being prepared to make a defense to anyone who asks you for a reason for the hope that is in you…

Once I took a group of men from my church on a Core Sound duck hunt that also provided us the opportunity to deer and dove hunt a friend's farm in Carteret County. We met at an agreed upon spot to pack the trucks and then divvy up between the vehicles for the six and a half hour drive to Harkers Island. What was amazing was how much gear and luggage ten men felt they needed.

Since we were going to try and do three different hunts, we did not travel light. Multiple shotguns, rifles, boxes of different ammo, waders, hunting boots, coolers, sleeping bags, blind bags and clothing were jammed into the beds of three trucks…barely. The joke was, "If we don't have it, you don't need it." Once we got to Harkers, we were glad for the overabundance of equipment.

Not only did three different types of hunting demand different types of gear, the weather was crazy – wind gusts up to 45 mph, temps fluctuating between high 30s to high 50s, rain the first half and sun the second. We needed everything we brought in order to meet the changing conditions. If we went after ducks on Core Sound in the rain, we were prepared. If we were sitting in a deer stand on a blustery sunny day, we had what we needed. Every situation, every condition was not a problem because we were ready.

This is the emphasis of I Peter 3:15. The apostle tells the early church (and us) to be ready to answer a non Christian's questions about why we believe what we believe and how our belief in Christ makes a difference in the everyday of life.

Notice the progression. First Christ must reign in our hearts. The word "holy" has at its core a sense of being unique, not common, different than everything else. So Christ is not seen as an add on to life. He is life, Lord, Master, Sovereign Ruler.

Next Peter tells us to be prepared, in other words, alert and watchful for the chance to show that Christ is consequential. We must be ready to give an answer when someone asks what difference Christ makes in our lives. Not a Sunday School, get-out-of-hell, Jesus wants us to be good kind of answer. Be ready to give a real, transparent, genuine reply that shows how the gospel has taken root in our souls and is seen in our actions and heard in our words.

How do we prepare? First, by submitting to the Lordship of Christ daily. Second, by diving deep in His truth. Third, by answering questions from those who are seeking. Finally, by making sure we are not intimidated by their questions and being willing to simply share what Christ has done for us.

So the next time you are getting ready for an outdoor excursion, ask yourself this question, "Do I take as much time and care in being ready to give a defense for my belief in Christ as I do when I head to the woods or water?"

Week 47
Answer Wisely

Prov. 15:1 A soft answer turns away wrath, but a harsh word stirs up anger.

Several years ago I had a group of guys duck hunting with me in Arkansas. Ox had once again graciously opened up his farms for us to make the long trek from North Carolina to the flooded fields of The Natural State.

The first couple of days were hard hunting. The ducks were spread out and just not cooperating with us. We were not getting skunked, but we were not even close to limiting out. As Mike and I scouted one day, we saw Gadwalls piling in to two fields on a neighboring farmer. I asked Mike whose land it was and he replied that it belonged to Mr. Phieffer. I asked if Mr. Phieffer would mind us hunting his property. Mike said he didn't think it would be a problem. He called for permission, and we were set to go after the hundreds of ducks that thought they had found a quiet spot.

Since there were two fields holding our quarry, we split up with one group going with Ox and one going with me. Our first hunt was in the afternoon so we arrived fairly early so we could have plenty of time to set out our decoys and find a good hidey-hole on the tree line.

As we were placing our decoys, I looked up and saw an Argo eight-wheeler piloted by two angry looking men tearing across the field toward us. I quickly deduced that we had accidently crossed over from Mr. Phieffer's property on to another duck lease. While the Argo was bearing down on us, I told my group I thought I had made a mistake and asked them to begin winding up the decs so we could move.

As soon as they came to a stop, I made the first move and said, "Guys have we accidently set up on your land?" They gruffly replied that we indeed were on their property. Instead of bowing up and answering them like they had spoken to me, I simply said, "I am really sorry. We didn't mean to mess ya'll up. We're hunting with Michael Oxner, and we have permission from Mr. Phieffer to try our luck on his land. We'll get our stuff moved right away." And do you know what? The demeanor of those men changed immediately. The anger and defensive mood melted away, and we began to have a nice chat about how their hunting season had gone.

Getting your back up and popping off, whether you are in the right or wrong, rarely calms down a situation. According to the Psalmist, it does just the opposite; harsh words are like gas on a fire; they do nothing but heat things up.

So the next time you are in a tense spot, take the time to ask God to calm your soul and quiet your mouth. You may be amazed at what happens when you do.

Week 48
An 8-Wheeler, Two Boys and A Stump

An Argo 8-Wheeler circa mid-1970's

Prov 26:18-19 Like a madman who throws firebrands, arrows, and death is a man who deceives his neighbor and says, 'I am only joking!'

A while back I was driving down Hwy 64 East headed to Tyrell County when I saw a camouflaged Argo sitting on the side of the road for sale. As soon as my eyes rested on this eight-wheel ATV, my mind went back many years to an incident that occurred with another Argo and a cypress stump.

Several of my running buddies had met at our hunting camp for a weekend of shooting guns, four-wheeling and exploring the bayou. Trey had begged his dad to let him bring their eight-wheeled Argo. For those of you who do not know what this is, it is an all terrain vehicle that floats. The machine is amazing as well as expensive, which is why Mr. Clifton was hesitant about us using it.

Now Trey had an interesting relationship with Michael Oxner. Basically, Ox would take advantage of Trey's trusting nature by stretching the truth. This occurred year after year until finally Trey decided he had had enough and was going to do exactly the opposite of what Michael said. The problem was he picked the wrong time to implement this plan.

Trey and Michael had hopped in the Argo and headed down a road that was cut decades ago when the bayou was being timbered. When winter came, the bayou flooded, which turned these paths into waterways through the trees. Ox was very familiar with the area so he knew where to go and where to avoid.

I stayed at the camper while they were exploring so I could get the gear in order. As I stepped outside, I heard an interesting combination of noises. One was the two-cycle engine of the Argo. Another was a person laughing so hard he was howling. The last one was a weird thumping sound. When the eight-wheeler came into view, I quickly saw that the thumping was from a bent axle, Michael was the source of the laughter and Trey was hollering at Ox to shut up.

When I finally got Trey to quit yelling at Michael and Michael to quit laughing, I found out what had happened. It seems they were motoring down the flooded logging road when Michael told Trey to turn left at a fork. Trey thought he was being set up, so he did exactly the opposite of what Ox was telling him, only to find out too late that Michael was being truthful this one time. Ox was trying to turn Trey away from a big cypress stump that was just under the surface of the water, but Trey didn't believe him and ran smack into it with such force that one of the four axles bent.

Don't kid so much that you lose credibility. Be a person of upright character so that when you tell your friend to turn left, he believes you.

Week 49
A Two Duck Dog

Col 3:23-24 Whatever you do, work heartily, as for the Lord and not for men; knowing that from the Lord you will receive the inheritance as your reward. You are serving the Lord Christ.

During the decades that I've duck hunted, I've seen a lot of changes in the world of water fowling. Shells going from lead to steel to now metal alloys with names I cannot pronounce, much less afford. Shells growing from 2 ¾ inch to 3 inch to now the uber-manly 3 ½ inch. Camo patterns that do not resemble any known tree or bush. I saw a time when the feds implemented a crazy point system for the daily bag limit. (They issued 100 points per day with different ducks assigned different values. A mallard hen = 100 points, a mallard drake = 75 and the lowly shoveler = 25.) I've even seen a dog that had a set number of ducks she would retrieve.

A farmer I worked for during the summer bought a yellow lab for bringing in his downed birds. The problem was that this dog was literally a two-duck dog. She had no problem hitting the water to go after the first bird. She even went hard after the second one was dropped. But, and this is the truth, that dog refused to retrieve anything after two.

The farmer would rant and rave and cuss, all with the same result; he ended up wading through the water to get his ducks while his dog stayed in the blind. Two ducks. That's it. No more. No less. No way was she going after number three.

That dog reminds me of me. I occasionally have a limit when it comes to obeying God. There are times that I read certain things in the Bible, and I am all over it. Truth just resonates in my soul, and I'm chomping at the bit to implement it. Then there are the times that I know truth, but I'm not all fired up about submitting to it. On some days I find myself acting kind of like that two-duck dog; I obey on my terms. I say, "God I'll do this, but my obedience only goes so far."

Now I'm not talking about heinous issues. I'm talking about everyday choices like speaking truth in a loving manner (Eph. 4:15), being ready to give an answer to those who ask me why I have hope (I Peter 3:15-16), not pushing my children to anger (Eph. 6:4) and praying for those who hate me (Matt. 5:44).

A dog that only retrieves two ducks is about worthless – just like a man who only obeys when he feels like it.

Do you find your response to God to be limited? In other words, will you go only so far in your obedience? What's keeping you from fully committing?

Week 50
Hey Man, Sorry About Shooting The Muzzleloader In The House

James 1:26 If anyone thinks he is religious and does not bridle his tongue but deceives his heart, this person's religion is worthless.

Sitting in my gun safe is a .50 caliber muzzleloader that has never killed anything but a shag carpet. Here's the story.

When Kimberly and I were married in 1989, my best man, Michael Oxner, thought it would be funny to give a Thompson New Englander muzzleloader to my wife and an ironing board to me as wedding gifts. Kimberly traded me even, so I ended up with the gun.

After our honeymoon, I took my newly acquired .50 to a friend's farm to sight it in. I poured in the powder, tapped in the ball, put on the cap, pulled the trigger and nothing, just the pop of the cap. I pulled the nipple, poured a little powder in the flash pan, put on a new cap, pulled the trigger and again, no shot. So now I had a fully loaded .50 caliber and no tools to pull the ball. This was way before breech-loading black powder guns.

We were still in college, so when I told Ox, he said to bring it back to school, and he had a tool that would remove the bullet. I took it over to the house he shared with two other friends and left it along with my supplies in his front room. Now my boy has always operated on his own timetable, so the gun sat for over a week in the same place that I left it.

One day another friend stopped by the house and saw the .50 propped in a corner. He also heard one of Ox's roommates snoring while taking an afternoon nap. This college student, not knowing the gun was charged, decided to put a cap on the nipple, sneak in beside Sleeping Beauty and pull the trigger thinking the noise of the cap would be a rude awakening.

So this guy slips in like Elmer Fudd going after Bugs Bunny, pulls the hammer back, points the barrel at the floor (thank the Lord), and blam the gun goes off, the boy taking a nap screams, stands straight up in the bed, and a hole the size of a small fist appears in the shag carpet.

Here is the point – that "friend" didn't mean to destroy the floor and scare the other guy by shooting a chunk of lead in the house. He didn't even know the muzzleloader was charged. However, intentions or ignorance did not mean a thing once the trigger was pulled. You can't get a bullet back after the powder goes off. Nor can you retrieve a hurtful word once it leaves your mouth. Be wise with what you say.

Have you done damage with your words recently? Are there some "holes in the floor" that you need to patch?

Week 51
Pink Holsters and Little Pistols

A young Paten listening for deer

1 Cor 16:13-14 Be watchful, stand firm in the faith, act like men, be strong. Let all that you do be done in love.

Many Christmases ago Oxner told me about an incident that occurred while his family opened presents. He and his wife gave each of their three children custom cap guns as one of their gifts. The two girls were to receive realistic chrome pieces housed in feminine pink holsters while their younger brother Paten was to get a smaller pistol.

The plan unraveled when the boy mistakenly unwrapped one of the girls' guns. He took out the pink-holstered six-shooter, stared at it and then yelled, "That's not mine! That's not mine!" His mother quickly saw the problem and told him he was right – that pistol wasn't his.

Relieved, the little tyke began to rip into his box only to discover his cap gun was much smaller than his siblings' guns. As he looked at his gift he asked, "Mommy did you buy this?" To which his mother replied she had. He then said, "I hate it!" It seemed neither a pink holster nor a pint-sized pistol appealed to his masculine side.

Even at a young age my friend's son had a picture of what it meant to be a man. Don't get bogged down on whether it was right or wrong to base his view on a pink holster and a smaller version of his sisters' guns. The fact is that at age five this boy had a vision of masculinity.

Our culture, the church included, has lost its way when it comes to raising boys to become Christ-honoring, Spirit-led, Bible-saturated men. The pendulum swings wildly between effeminate, emotionally-led males to knuckle-dragging, back-scratching Neanderthals, neither of which is God's design.

Look at what Paul writes to the men at Corinth.

- **Be watchful and stand firm in the faith** – These commands have a military ring. As John Piper teaches, life is war so be ready for the enemy. And when the attacks come, don't give ground. Dig in knowing that our faith in Christ ultimately overcomes everything we face.
- **Act like men** – God created us as men so don't apologize for or take pride in being men. Simply do life on His terms.
- **Be strong** – Take the lead; be courageous; be selfless; don't be passive.
- **Do everything in love** – Paul wraps it up with a great phrase. All that is done must be couched in terms of "agape"; that God-exalting, self-giving love that seeks the benefit of others. Not the emotional sappy stuff of Hallmark movies, but strong sacrificial choices that build up.

Take each of those four underlined statements and rank yourself 1-5 on how you are doing. (1 = striking out 5 = hitting homeruns) What are some actions you can take to shore up the areas where you are weak?

Week 52
The End

Eccles. 1:4 A generation goes, and a generation comes...

In January of 2013, I headed to Brinkley for an extended time of duck hunting. I hosted several friends at my mom and dad's house while they were away in Belize on a mission trip. That all sounds pedestrian, nothing out of the ordinary. And you would be right except for the fact that this would be the last time I slept in the house that my parents had called home for 42 years.

Dad retired from the ministry in December of 2012. He faithfully served his Lord and the people of Brinkley, Arkansas for 42 years. During that time he and mom raised a family at 315 South Main, the address for a red brick ranch-style parsonage. My siblings and I had never known another house. That was about to change.

I loved going back to my parents' house, seeing and hearing the familiar, getting up to hunt at o-dark-thirty and not having to turn on any lights because I knew that house like the back of my hand. Two steps from the bed, reach with my right hand and find the door knob; walk into the hallway and turn right, five steps and I'm at the door to the den; turn left then six steps to the right where coffee is waiting in the kitchen; walk through to the mudroom where I laid out my gear the night before. All the while as I walk in the dark, I hear the loud ticking of both the mantle clock on the shelf in the den and the wall clock hanging in the living room. In the background my ear catches the lonely whistle of the freight train coming through Brinkley – a whistle that I've heard for 43 years.

And now? That house with its memories will be gone. It's all changing, and I can't help but be a little sad and nostalgic. Coming back to my hometown will never be the same because that which has been familiar is gone. Another pastor and his family occupy the house where we were raised. It just happens. A generation goes, and a generation comes.

Solomon's father, King David, prayed that God would teach him to number his days. Make the most of the time God gives because it passes all too quickly.

How do you want to be remembered? If you died today, how do you think you would be remembered?

ABOUT THE AUTHOR

A native Arkansan, Joel McDaniel is a graduate of The University of Arkansas and Southwestern Baptist Theological Seminary. He has served as a pastor for over 25 years. Joel and his wife Kimberly currently reside in Raleigh, NC where he is a teaching pastor at Capital Community Church and the executive director of Operation Resolute, a ministry dedicated to serving active duty military.

34603209R00061

Made in the USA
Columbia, SC
16 November 2018